Evangelism and Social Involvement

EVANGELISM AND SOCIAL INVOLVEMENT

BROADMAN PRESS
Nashville, Tennessee

© Copyright 1986 • Broadman Press
All rights reserved
4262-48
ISBN: 0-8054-6248-1
Dewey Decimal Classification: 269
Subject Headings: EVANGELISM
Library of Congress Catalog Card Number: 86-2660
Printed in the United States of America

Scripture quotations are from the Revised Standard Version of the Bible, copyrighted 1946, 1952, © 1971, 1973.

Library of Congress Cataloging-in-Publication Data

Miles, Delos.
  Evangelism and social involvement.

  Bibliography: p.
  Includes index.
  1. Evangelistic work. 2. Church and social problems. 3. Church and the world. I. Title.
BV3793.M45   1986   269'.2   86-2660
ISBN 0-8054-6248-1

To the church of my childhood and youth, Bethel Baptist Church, Rt. 1, Olanta, S. C., with eternal thanks to God and everlasting gratitude to you for all that you have done for me. You led me to Christ; nurtured me in the faith; taught me my first lessons in evangelism and social involvement; licensed and ordained me to the gospel ministry; encouraged me through long years of study and preparation; and have prayed for me for more than forty years.

Preface

Evangelist Billy Graham defined evangelism in 1983 as "the offering of the whole Christ, by the whole Church, to the whole man, to the whole world."[1] If the world-renowned evangelist was right, and I believe he was, then evangelism and social involvement are two wings of the same gospel bird.

Evangelism and Christian social concern are two sides of the same coin. If one side of a coin is missing, that coin has lost its value. The lack of a social conscience impugns the reputation of the holy God and leads to societal failure. Evangelism is surely a blood brother to social involvement.

Perhaps we need something like physicist Nils Bohr's 1927 Theory of Complementarity in physics to help us view the essential wholeness of the gospel.[2] E. Stanley Jones, an indefatigable evangelist, said: "An individual gospel without a social gospel is a soul without a body, and a social gospel without an individualized gospel is a body without a soul. One is a ghost and the other is a corpse."[3]

We haven't yet learned that what happens in Washington, D. C., and Wake Forest, North Carolina, and everywhere else is related to what happens in every human heart. The confession, "Jesus is Lord," repudiates any bifurcation between one's personal and public life.

Jesus had no problem coupling evangelism and service. It is a warped gospel which does not cover the gamut of human need. The Sunday School Jesus may confine Himself to changing persons' hearts, but the Jesus of the Gospels aimed at changing human hearts and human society.

Mother Theresa of India has been reported to say that it is easier to feed the hungry millions in India than to deal with spiritual poverty in America. Another has asserted that it is easier to proclaim the unsearchable riches of God in a Communist nation than in America. I do not believe the latter statement for a moment. In fact, I take strong exception to it. Nevertheless, I do believe that our spiritual poverty frequently hinders us from viewing evangelism and social involvement as legitimate partners.

Jerry Falwell has spoken of the weaknesses of Fundamentalism in regard to social involvement. "We tend to be negative and pessimistic," said Falwell. "We have been irresponsible as Christian citizens. We have almost totally avoided the political process and the social life of our country." Then, Falwell continued, "We have neglected reaching the whole person for the cause of Christ."[4] Falwell's indictments apply also to many Christians who may prefer to call themselves Evangelicals.

Inasmuch as many have addressed the relationship between evangelism and social involvement, you may wonder why I should presume to write on the interfacing of the two. Most of those who have addressed the linkage have been persons in ethics, history, journalism, or missiology. My perspective is that of an evangelist and one who has committed his life to the teaching of evangelism. For more than two decades of my professional life, I have self-consciously sought to find out how evangelism and social involvement should be related.

Suffice it to say at the outset that my friend Robert Hamblin, who heads the evangelism program of Southern Baptists, spoke my sentiments when he said:

> I feel social ministry and evangelism are inseparable. I've never believed social ministry is evangelism, but social ministry can and should be evangelistic. Neither do I believe we should do social ministries to evangelize. We should do social ministries because we love people and want to meet their needs.[5]

I owe a special debt of gratitude to my wife, Nada, for typing the manuscript so patiently and quickly. John Marion Adams, my grader and research assistant, did the painstaking work on the indexes. Larry L. Rose, executive director of the Center for Urban Church Studies in Nashville, gave me valuable advice and encouragement. Dale W. Cross, director of metropolitan evangelism strategy for Southern Baptists in Atlanta, made helpful suggestions and provided some materials through the Evangelism Section of the Home Mission Board of the Southern Baptist Convention.

Most of the on-site research for the writing was done during a half-year sabbatical from my teaching duties. I am grateful to President W. Randall Lolley, Dean Morris Ashcraft, and the trustees of Southeastern Baptist Theological Seminary for their generosity.

Notes

1. Billy Graham, "The Evangelist and a Torn World," *Decision*, vol. 24, no. 11, November, 1983, p. 2 of insert "Special Report on Amsterdam 83."

2. The theory or principle of complementarity posited by Nils Bohr states that the wave and particle models of either matter or radiation complement each other. Neither model may be used exclusively to adequately describe matter or radiation. Only when the two models are combined in a complementary manner can a complete understanding be obtained. This theory helps us to deal with the problem of understanding the dual nature of both matter and radiation conceptually, because the two models appear to contradict each other. Bohr's theory has proven especially useful in quantum mechanics. See J. Rud Nielsen, ed., *Nils Bohr Collected Works*, Vol. 1, (Amsterdam: Worth-Holland Publishing Co., 1972), pp. XL-XLI; see also: Raymond A. Serway, *Physics: For Scientists and Engineers* (Philadelphia: Saunders College Publishing, 1982), p. 875.

3. Quoted by Arthur L. Beals, "Of Ghosts and Corpses," *Seeds*, vol. 5, no. 8, August, 1982, p. 25.

4. Jerry Falwell, "Why I Am a Fundamentalist," *Fundamentalist Journal*, vol. 1, no. 1, September, 1982, p. 6.

5. Quoted by Jim Newton, "Bob Hamblin Relational Evangelist," *Missions USA*, Nov.-Dec., 1982, vol. 53, no. 6, p. 56.

Contents

1. **Introduction** **13**
   The Great Divide • Meaning of Terms • Bridge Over Troubled Waters

Section I. Foundational Interfaces

2. **Biblical Origins** **27**
   The Two Mandates • Other Old Testament Passages • The Healing Ministry of Jesus • The Mission of Jesus • The Rich Man and Lazarus • The Judgment of the Nations • Other New Testament Passages

3. **Historical Roots** **38**
   The Early Church • Modern Missions • The Clapham Sect • The Second Great Awakening • The Confessing Church of Germany

4. **Theological Sources** **55**
   Creation • Sin • *Agape*

Section II. Contemporary Interfaces

5. **Examples of Individual Christians Building Bridges** **69**
   The Example of Dru Graves • The Example of Hubert Line • The Example of Don Stanley • The Example of Jim Fuller • The Example of Bob Hoehn • The Example of John Hendrix • The Example of Sam and Ginny Cannata

6. **Examples of Local Churches Building Bridges** **81**
   Bronx Baptist Church, Bronx • Hominy Baptist Church, Candler • Collage of Churches

7. **Examples of Parachurch Organizations Building Bridges** **102**
   Christian Rehabilitation Center, Charlotte • Emmanuel Gospel Center, Boston • Voice of Calvary Ministries, Jackson

8. **Six Models for Naming the Name of Jesus** **125**
   The Traditional-Rescue-Mission Approach • The Risky-Deed-and-Word Approach • The U. C. - J. C. Approach • The Never-on-Friday-the-Thirteenth Approach • The Specialization Approach • The Conversion-of-Structures Approach

Section III. Future Interfaces

9. **Point-of-Need Evangelism** **135**
   A Typology of Personal Evangelism • Commentary on the

Typology • The Typology Illuminated by Two Cases • Point-of-Need Type Illustrated • The Evangelism of Jesus

10. **Prophetic Evangelism** **145**
    Connecting Evangelism and Prophecy • One Model Described and Critiqued • Two Very Different Models • Values of Prophetic Evangelism

11. **Advice for Christian Social Ministers and Evangelists** **155**
    Advice for Christian Social Ministers • Advice for Evangelists • Advice for Both

    Annotated Bibliography **167**

    Indexes **181**
    Scripture Index • General Index

1
Introduction

Scripture Lesson: Isaiah 61:1-11; Luke 4:16-30

The Great Divide

Perhaps you have heard the apocryphal story which illustrates the two main schools of thought regarding evangelism and social action. It tells of evangelism hamburgers made of rabbit and elephant—one elephant and one rabbit. The evangelism hamburger on the left is made of one social action elephant and one evangelism rabbit. The one on the right is composed of one evangelism elephant and one social action rabbit. Donald McGavran sees the evangelism hamburger on the left being offered to the public by the World Council of Churches, and the evangelism hamburger on the right being offered by the Lausanne Committee on World Evangelization.[1]

That story is also indicative of the great divide which exists today between evangelism and social involvement. For example, the leader of a major Protestant denomination in a message on Hebrews 2:3 warned his denomination in 1982 against the social gospel.[2]

Evidently this leader sincerely believes that salvation is radically set against the social gospel. Apparently he cannot agree with Nazarene scholar Timothy Smith's thesis in *Revivalism and Social Reform* that the social gospel had its origins in the doctrine of sanctification and the methods of mass evangelism *after* 1842.[3]

Evangelicals are deeply concerned that as some Christians move toward greater social involvement they seem to correspondingly move away from biblical Christianity. Sherwood Eliot Wirt raises the issue this way: "What is there in the present age that seems to make it mandatory for a man to move from orthodoxy to atheism before he can be taken seriously in his quest for the good of humanity?"[4]

Sociologist Dean R. Hoge in a book review said categorically, "Today the social-action controversy is over...." Hoge thinks those in favor of social action lost the war. Later, in that same review, he wrote: "Most people have apparently accepted Dean Kelley's view that Protestant churches lack the organizational strength to undertake significant social action."[5]

I do not believe for a moment that an adequate bridge of reconciliation has been built across these troubled waters of evangelism and social involvement. The great divide is still there in spite of all our best efforts to bridge over it. Nevertheless, I believe that this great canyon is bridged in the Bible, that it can be bridged through Christ, and that it is basically a twentieth-century phenomenon which is the result of what David O. Moberg calls "The Great Reversal."[6]

This volume is one of my efforts to reverse "the great reversal," and to do my part as an evangelist and a teacher to construct a more permanent bridge over the great divide of evangelism and Christian social involvement. I am conscious of building upon the labors of others. Some of these previous bridge builders are credited in the notes and in the bibliography.

Meaning of Terms

Several terms need to be defined and clarified before we can proceed. The first of these is *evangelism*.

Evangelism

Evangelism is being, doing, and telling the gospel of the kingdom of God, in order that by the power of the Holy Spirit persons and structures may be converted to the lordship of Jesus Christ. This definition sees evangelization as a three dimensional phenomenon having to do with being, doing, and telling the good news about God's reign over the universe through Christ. It views evangelism as a kingdom-of-God enterprise. Therefore, evangelism has both a personal and corporate dimension.

Introduction

This definition lifts up evangelism as a work of the Holy Spirit. God's Spirit is the great Enabler in all evangelization. The discerning eye will also gaze upon the intentionality of evangelism in the definition. Evangelism has a razor-sharp cutting edge to it. Its intention is to convert persons and structures to the lordship of Jesus Christ. It does not apologize for wanting to disciple all the peoples of the planet.

Some missiologists prefer the European definition of evangelism as evangelization, which stresses exposure to the gospel in its most rudimentary form as evangelism. The European understanding of evangelization clearly differentiates between evangelism and conversion. The American school tends more to identify evangelism with conversion. You can see a classic expression of the European view in David B. Barrett's massive and revolutionary *World Christian Encyclopedia*. Barrett, using the European view of evangelism, projects that 83.4 percent of the world will be evangelized by the year 2000. Even D. A. McGavran labels that estimate "hopelessly optimistic."[7]

The evangelism which we prize is not just the strong, clear proclamation of the gospel of Jesus Christ. It also involves an intentional Christian presence and a dialogical persuasion. Instead of counting decisions, it counts disciples. Responsible membership in the body of Christ is what we are after. We want real Christians instead of "rice" Christians.

Let us, however, not entertain any illusions about converting structures to the lordship of Jesus Christ. Some entire family structures can be converted. To deny that would be to deny the examples of complete households being saved in the New Testament. But the conversion of most corporate structures is an exceedingly complex matter.

Christians are not apt to change larger social and political structures in those lands and communities where they are a tiny minority. In fact, until they number in excess of 10 percent about the only structures they can change are their own families and neighborhoods.[8]

I know that talk about the conversion of structures may

be strange to most of us. Such language recognizes the corporate nature of society, the corporate dimension of sin and evil, and the corporate character of the kingdom of God. We draw back from it because of our Western ideology of rugged individualism, our evangelical captivity to private faith, and our blindness to corporate personality in the Bible.

In chapter 3, I shall single out the abolition of slavery as a prime example of the conversion of structures. Poverty, witchcraft, prostitution, child labor, war, abortion, pornography, racism, sexism, and ageism are but a few examples of other sinful structures which Christians have sought to convert to the lordship of Jesus Christ. If you prefer some other terms like *transformation* or *change* rather than *conversion,* I shall not quibble with you so long as you seek to do justice to the biblical concept of corporateness.

Social Ministry and Social Action

Two terms which are frequently used in speaking about Christian social involvement are *social ministry* and *social action*. Social ministry is feeding the hungry, giving drink to the thirsty, welcoming strangers, clothing the naked, and visiting the sick and the prisoners. In other words, social ministry is doing such deeds of love and mercy as those mentioned four times in the judgment of the nations scene in Matthew 25:31-46.

Christian social action, on the other hand, involves self-conscious attempts to change sinful social structures. Social action includes deeds of love and justice on behalf of society's outcasts and underclasses. Such actions may range all the way from passing a resolution to participating in an armed revolution, although many Christians will draw a line before the use of violence and some before the breaking of any laws.

The good Samaritan story of Luke 10:25-37 may illustrate the difference between social ministry and social action. What the good Samaritan did was social ministry. If he had sought to change the conditions which led to the Jericho road robbery and mugging, that would have been social action.

Introduction

T. B. Maston, a retired professor of ethics, used the analogy of a precipice to illustrate what we need to do in the way of social involvement. "We want to provide an ambulance at the foot of the precipice," said Maston. That is Christian social ministry to the wounded victims. But we also "want to build a fence and set up warning signals at the top of the precipice," the professor continued. That is Christian social action.

A part of the great debate in the church this century has to do with whether it is appropriate for churches as organizations to engage in social action. Most of them are involved to some extent in social ministry. Some of them are involved in social action. But many well-meaning Christians think it inappropriate for churches as churches to be engaged in social action. Yet even those are usually willing for their members to be engaged in social action as individual Christians or as members of nonchurch or parachurch organizations.

The social action involvement of large numbers of fundamentalists and conservative Christians in the 1980 American presidential election came as a surprise to many more liberal church leaders. Especially were they shocked by the leadership role of fundamentalist and conservative pastors. The right wing of the American church flexed its growing political muscles in 1980 and again in 1984. Apparently the kind of social action which the religious right represents is a new political fact with which all politicians must wrestle in this decade. It is important, however, to note that the primary vehicle for such social action is nonchurch and parachurch organizations rather than local churches or denominations.

One additional point which needs to be made about social action is that churches as churches, denominational boards, agencies, and judicatories have often been involved in social action throughout American church history. The same denomination whose previously mentioned leader spoke so negatively against the social gospel passed resolutions on abortion, alcohol, Sunday football, prayers in public schools, peace, and unethical newspaper reporting. It discussed, but

Evangelism and Social Involvement

postponed a resolution affirming the nation Israel. Ironically, the resolution on Israel came during the very time when Israel had invaded Lebanon, an invasion which resulted in 600,000 homeless persons and the death of up to 9,500 civilians.[9]

Development, Relief, and Rehabilitation

Increasingly the term *development* is coming into our vocabulary on social involvement. "In the short time since 1970, relief organizations have established a new science, recorded a history, and presented a literature," wrote J. Alan Youngren. That new science is called "development." Actually there are three technical terms used in connection with development.

Development is "the science of encouraging economic and social progress that is self-sustaining." *Relief* brings an end to the suffering and other effects of a crisis or disaster. *Rehabilitation* restores the community to the stable circumstances which prevailed before the crisis. Whereas rehabilitation and development are sometimes used interchangeably, the preferred term is *development;* it is used to refer also to that third stage in the process which enables the community to better itself and attain a new self-sufficiency. Functionally, relief organizations describe this work as relief, rehabilitation, and development.[10]

Development is big business. Total revenue given for relief in the USA is many millions as reflected in the following table:

Revenue Summary
(in millions of dollars)

Organization	1978	1979	1980
World Relief	1.5	4.2	13.7
Food for the Hungry	2.9	3.9	6.7
World Vision	39.3	46.7	80.0
World Concern	1.8	2.6	3.9
MAP International	9.6	13.8	27.9
Compassion		7.5	(est.)10.9[11]

Admittedly, relief organizations can't raise funds by talking about development. Most of them are still caught up in the naked-child syndrome. Donors prefer to adopt a particular child rather than a village or community. Nevertheless, *development* is rapidly becoming the technical umbrella term for Christian social ministry and social action—especially as practiced by religious or quasireligious organizations working beyond the local churches and overseas.

Bridge Over Troubled Waters

Now that we have viewed the great divide and defined our terms, how shall we bring the broken parts together?

The World Evangelical Fellowship and the Lausanne Committee for World Evangelization jointly sponsored a six-day meeting in 1982 at Reformed Bible College in Grand Rapids, Michigan, to consider the relationship between evangelism and social responsibility. Over fifty evangelical theolgians from twenty-six countries participated. The meeting was not to rewrite but to clarify the statement in the Lausanne Covenant concerning the responsibility of Christians to engage in social and political action.

A number of pressing questions were addressed. What kind of balance is desirable between evangelism and social justice? Which, if either, should have priority? How may the church minister to the spiritual and physical needs of a troubled world? How should the evangelical Christian respond to the insistent demands of liberation theologians that Christians join in the struggle for social justice?

Eight major papers and case studies were presented. These considered ways in which Christians through the centuries have viewed evangelism and social action, how eschatological views may influence social action, and the propriety of using salvation language to describe social or political liberation.

That 1982 meeting stoutly affirmed the priority of evangelism:

> Evangelism has a logical priority.... If social action is a consequence and aim of evangelism (as we have asserted) then evangelism must precede it.... Seldom if ever should

we have to choose between satisfying physical hunger and spiritual hunger, or between healing bodies and saving souls, since an authentic love for our neighbor will lead us to serve him or her as a whole person. Nevertheless, if we must choose, then we have to say that the supreme and ultimate need of all mankind is the saving grace of Jesus Christ and therefore a person's eternal, spiritual salvation is of greater importance than his or her temporal and material well-being.[12]

The official Grand Rapids report identified three relationships between the two disciplines as "equally valid." These are: social concern as a consequence of evangelism; social concern as a bridge to evangelism; and social concern as a partner of evangelism.[13]

Evangelist Leighton Ford has set forth several options for social responsibility as it relates to evangelism. Social responsibility is variously seen as:
- a *distraction* from evangelism ("Why shift furniture when the house is burning?");
- a *result* of evangelism ("Changed people will change the world");
- a *preparation* for evangelism ("Hungry people can't listen to sermons");
- a *partner* of evangelism;
- an *essential element* of evangelism;
- an *equivalent* of evangelism.[14]

Let us briefly look at statements by four churchmen and see if we can discover where they might fit into Ford's options.

Karl Barth explicitly disavowed that the work of the church was to improve society.[15] What Barth seemed to mean was that the existence of the church rests not in its outward activity but in its focus on the presence of God. If on the basis of that word, we had to force Barth into one of the options, we might conclude that he saw social involvement as a distraction from evangelism.

Browne Barr seems to be following Barth when he cautions us against measuring and judging the church by its "doing" rather than by its "being." When we measure the church by its doing,

Its existence centers on its achievement. Is it growing? Is it extending its influence for good? Is it an effective agent for social change? Is it helping to enrich family life? Is it attentive to the needs of the oppressed? Is it an instrument for the liberation of the bound? All of these questions, I suggest are pressingly crucial and legitimate, but they are secondary nontheless. They derive from the being of the church and do not define it.... We must ask first not "What does the church do," but "What is the church?"[16]

Bishop William R. Cannon, who was chairman of the World Methodist Council in 1981, identified the biggest issue facing the Methodist Church as evangelism. "We forget that, due to the pressures of so many social problems on us," said Cannon. "Even if you secure good and just institutions for society, they aren't going to hold up unless you have the good, moral spirit of people to operate on."[17] Bishop Cannon in those words seems to view social involvement as a result of evangelism.

Later in a keynote episcopal address to his denomination's 1984 quadrennial church conference, the United Methodist bishop clearly identified himself with those who view social involvement as a result of evangelism. He explained his denomination's loss of 1.5 million members in the last twenty years in terms of dealing with social structures versus evangelizing people. "We have spent much time dealing with social structures ... and far too little time evangelizing people," said the bishop. Bishop Cannon went on to explain that while the church had done much to improve the lot of people, it lately "had done far too little to save their souls. If our losses continue as they have been, there will not be members left in the United States to implement the social programs of which we are so proud."[18]

"To truncate the Christian mission simply to the changing of social structures," said Carl F. H. Henry, "profoundly misunderstands the biblical view of human nature and divine redemption."[19] I heartily agree. If that kind of reductionism does happen, we could lose sight of the individual persons for whom all social structures exist. Nevertheless, I should argue just as strongly that to truncate the Christian mission simply to the changing of individual persons profoundly misunderstands the biblical view of sin and of the demonic powers and principalities as well as the biblical view of the kingdom of God.

Henry sees social responsibility as a result of evangelism and as a partner. It might even be a preparation for evangelization. But, he also recognizes the possibility of social involvement becoming an illegitimate substitute for evangelism. That is probably what Ford has in mind when he cites the option of seeing social responsibility as an equivalent of evangelism.

My personal view is that social involvement and evangelism are partners. If you would see evangelism and social involvement in partnership, look at how Jesus combined the two in His life and ministry. His ministry was characterized by both proclamation (*kerygma*) and service (*diaconia*). The two went hand in hand, with His words explaining His works, and His works dramatizing His words. His words and deeds were expressions of compassion for persons.

There are times when social involvement is a preparation for evangelism. Wherever evangelism occurs, social involvement should follow until the second coming. I also see social involvement as an essential element of authentic evangelism. But I do not believe social involvement is a distraction from evangelism. Nor do I believe it should ever become an equivalent of evangelism.

The gospel of the kingdom of God is compromised and caricatured by those who reduce it to the changing of social structures or to the changing of individual persons. The evangelist is a change agent for God out to change persons and to change society. The evangelist deals first and foremost with that profound change which the Bible calls repentance and reconciliation. And neither repentance or reconciliation is a private transaction. Both are relational and have huge social consequences.

I am painfully aware that there are those among us whose rhetoric may lead us to believe that evangelism and Christian social involvement do not meet each other, let alone

Introduction

mix together. Nevertheless, I contend that the two should and do, in fact, interface.

The interfacing which occurs when tongue and groove lumber is fitted together in the construction of a house may provide an apt analogy. Tongued and grooved lumber, when properly fitted together, form such an entity that each piece complements and completes the other.

Conclusion

There is a sense in which what we are talking about is the connection between evangelism and ethics. What is the link between evangelism and ethics? One writer sees evangelism as *proclaiming* the gospel of reconciliation and ethics as *applying* that gospel. Christ brought both together in the Great Commission of Matthew 28.

Is evangelism preethics, or is ethics preevangelism? If evangelism is preethics, then the application of the gospel automatically follows its acceptance. If ethics is preevangelism, then the application of the gospel precedes its proclamation and prepares persons to receive it.

Some persons think Bob Dylan's conversion is based on a dollar sign, that he is simply cashing in on a good thing. Maybe so, but as Charles J. Bussey says: "Such an analysis seems . . . unsatisfactory; Dylan's concern for justice has been consistent throughout his career. Christianity is simply a logical extension of his long-term themes. In most cases, Charles Colson's for example, ethics follow conversion; in Dylan's life it was just the reverse."[20]

What about a third alternative, namely that evangelism is ethics and ethics is evangelism? That would mean that the application and proclamation of the gospel are synonomous.[21] I like the idea of the two working together, but I do not believe the two are one and the same. Each however is certainly dependent upon the other. Foy Valentine expressed my view of the two, when after thirty years of work in the area of the Christian life, he said: "I believe that no greater heresy has ever beset the Christian church than that which has separated evangelism from ethics, faith from works, words from deeds."[22]

24
Evangelism and Social Involvement

Notes

1. See Donald McGavran, "Credible and Authentic Evangelism," *Global Church Growth Bulletin*, Sept.-Oct., 1980, vol. XVII, no. 5, p. 63.

2. See an address by President Bailey E. Smith to the Southern Baptist Convention, June 15, 1982, in New Orleans.

3. Timothy L. Smith, *Revivalism and Social Reform* (New York: Abingdon Press, 1957), especially pp. 148-162, chapter X, "The Evangelical Origins of Social Christianity."

4. Sherwood Eliot Wirt, *The Social Conscience of the Evangelical* (New York: Harper & Row, Publishers, 1968), p. 41.

5. See Dean R. Hoge's review of James R. Wood's *Leadership in Voluntary Organizations: The Controversy Over Social Action in Protestant Churches* (Rutgers University Press) in *The Christian Century*, vol. 99, no. 23, July 7-14, 1982, pp. 764-765.

6. See David O. Moberg, *The Great Reversal: Evangelism and Social Concern* (Philadelphia: J. B. Lippincott Co., 1977, rev. ed.), especially pp. 28-45.

7. See Harry Genet's review of David B. Barrett's *World Christian Encyclopedia* (Oxford University Press, 1982), "Why Christian Nose Counting Boggles the Mind," *Christianity Today*, vol. XXVI, no. 11, June 18, 1982, pp. 76-77.

8. See D. A. McGavran's editorial note, "Postscript to Leighton Ford," *Global Church Growth Bulletin*, vol. XIX, no. 3, May-June, 1982, p. 184.

9. See *Newsweek*, June 28, 1982, p. 22. Later, the Red Cross reported that 14,000 people had died and 20,000 had been wounded. See also, "Residents Told to Flee from Beirut," *The News and Observer*, June 28, 1982, pp. 1A and 10A, Raleigh, N. C.

10. See J. Alan Youngren, "The Shell Game Donors Love to Lose," *Christianity Today*, vol. XXVI, no. 11, June 18, 1982, pp. 39-41. More recently among some Evangelicals the term *transformation* has gained favor over *development*. See Wayne Bragg, "Beyond Development," in *The Church in Response to Human Need* Tom Sine, ed. (Monrovia, CA.: Missions Advanced Research and Communication Center, 1983), pp. 37-95 and especially pp. 71-84. I also recommend to those readers who desire a fuller, evangelical perspective on development: Robert Lincoln Hancock, ed. and Carl F. H. Henry, convenor, *The Ministry of Development in Evangelical Perspective: A Symposium on the Social and Spiritual Mandate* (Pasadena, CA.: William Carey Library, 1979), 109 pp.

11. Youngren, p. 40.

12. See Arthur Williamson, "Evangelicals Study the Link Between Social Action and Gospel," *Christianity Today*, vol. XXVI, no. 13, Aug. 6, 1982, pp. 54 and 56. A full report on the 1982 Grand Rapids meeting is available in Lausanne Occasional Papers No. 21 Grand Rapids Report, *Evangelism and Social Responsibility: An Evangelical Commitment*, 1982, a joint publication of the Lausanne Committee for World Evangelization and the World Evangelical Fellowship.

13. Ibid., p. 56.

14. Leighton Ford, "Evangelism and Social Responsibility," *World Evangelization*, Information Bulletin No. 26, March, 1982, p. 6.

15. Cited by Richard G. Hutcheson, Jr., *Wheel Within the Wheel* (Atlanta: John Knox Press, 1979), p. 66.

16. See Browne Barr, "Name Tags and the Theocentric Focus," The *Christian Century*, XCVII, no. 38, Nov. 26, 1980, p. 1159.

Introduction

17. See John Robinson, "N. C. Bishop Goes Far in Calling," *The News and Observer,* Raleigh, N. C., Sept. 27, 1981, p. 29-I.

18. AP report, "Methodist Leaders Urge United Force," *The Augusta Chronicle,* Augusta, Ga., May 9, 1984, p. 6A.

19. Carl F. H. Henry, "American Evangelicals in a Turning Time," *The Christian Century,* vol. XCVII, no. 35, Nov. 5, 1980, p. 1062.

20. See Daniel Vestal, "An Agenda for Evangelism and Ethics: Bold Mission Thrust," *Light,* Nov., 1981, pp. 2 and 10. *Light* is a publication of the Christian Life Commission of the Southern Baptist Convention (S.B.C.)

21. Charles J. Bussey, "Bob Dylan: Driven Home," *Christianity Today,* vol. XXV, no. 12, June 26, 1981, p. 48.

22. See the interview, "Thirty Years Helping Changed People Change the World," *Light,* March-April, 1983, p. 2.

Section I
Foundational Interfaces

2
Biblical Origins

Scripture Lesson: Genesis 1:26-31; Matthew 28:16-20

One permanent temptation for us Christians, according to a French poet, is to pray the "Our Father" this way: "Our Father, who art in heaven—remain there."[1] Biblically literate Christians know they can't pray that way.

Evangelism and social involvement have many interfaces in the Bible. Let us examine some of those tie-ins.

The Cultural and Evangelistic Mandates

First, see how evangelism and social involvement fit together in the cultural and evangelistic mandates of Scripture. We sometimes forget that there are two great mandates in the Bible.

The cultural mandate is first recorded in Genesis 1:26-31.[2] Adam and Eve were given dominion, or delegated sovereignty, over the whole creation. They are commanded by God to "be fruitful and multiply, and fill the earth and subdue it; and have dominion over . . . every living thing" (Gen. 1:28).

The evangelistic mandate is usually associated with the Great Commission of Matthew 28:16-20. The new humanity in Christ (i.e., the church), is commanded by the risen Lord to make disciples of all nations. The crucial part of the evangelistic mandate reads:

> All authority in heaven and on earth has been given to me. Go therefore and make disciples of all nations, baptizing them in the name of the Father and of the Son and of the Holy Spirit, teaching them to observe all that I have commanded you; and lo, I am with you always, to the close of the age (Matt. 28:18-20).

The cultural mandate antedates the evangelistic mandate. Neither has ever been rescinded. They are both still binding upon us. As a matter of fact, we encounter that cultural mandate in the New Testament in the form of the Great Commandment. The Great Commandment says: "You shall love the Lord your God with all your heart, and with all your soul, and with all your mind. This is the great and first commandment. And a second is like it, You shall love your neighbor as yourself. On these two commandments depend all the law and the prophets" (Matt. 22:37-40).

If the Great Commission is our evangelistic mandate and the Great Commandment our ethical and social mandate, as some conveniently identify them, two strong points may be made immediately about their interfacing. The same one who gave the Great Commission also gave the Great Commandment. And both of them are found in the same Gospel of Matthew. We may fittingly add: "What God has joined together, let not persons put asunder."

Certainly one of the biblical areas where evangelism and Christian social involvement interface is in the Great Commission and the Great Commandment. Love for neighbor is surpassed only by our love for God. Nevertheless, the proof positive of our love for God is the concrete love which we show to our neighbor.

The Great Commission says, "make disciples of all nations," whereas the Great Commandment says in effect, "love God supremely and neighbor as self." These two mandates are on a par with each other. Neither one supercedes or exhausts or explains the other.

Our Lord's evangelism was not like Ephraim, a half-baked cake, done on one side and raw on the other (Hos. 7:8). His disciple making was characterized by an inseparable connection between evangelism and ethics.

I believe it is a theological mistake to identify either the Great Commission or the Great Commandment exclusively with either evangelism or ethics. If we love God with our whole being, we cannot help but share that consuming love with our lost neighbors. If we love our neighbors and they are hungry for the bread of life, we shall doubtlessly tell them about the bread of life which we have found in Jesus Christ. That may be what Paul meant when he said, "the love of Christ controls us" (2 Cor. 5:14).

John Masefield has a couplet in "The Everlasting Mercy" which seems to sum up the love for neighbor part of the Great Commandment:

> I knew that Christ had given me birth
> To brother all the souls on earth.

Then, too, one of the ways in which the Great Commission commands us to make disciples is by "teaching them to observe all that I have commanded you" (Matt. 28:20). Certainly, that would include what Jesus called "the great and first commandment" and the second commandment which is like the first (see Matt. 22:38-39). If all of the law and the prophets depend on these two commandments (see Matt. 22:40), we dare not ignore them in our disciple making.

So, our neighbor love cannot stop either with the meeting of heart needs, body needs, or head needs. "Our neighbour is neither a bodyless soul that we should love only his soul," says John R. W. Stott, "nor a soulless body that we should care for its welfare alone; nor even a body-soul isolated from society." Indeed, as Stott continues, "God created man, who is my neighbour a body-soul-in-community. Therefore if we love our neighbour as God made him, we must inevitably be concerned for his total welfare—the good of his soul, his body, and his community."[3]

"The biblical evidence overwhelmingly states that the will of God is to love him in a way that leaves no room for idols," said John Perkins, "and to love our neighbor in a way that liberates him from poverty and oppression either spiritual or physical."[4]

Before we go on to look at another place where the Bible ties together evangelism and social involvement, it is important to note that both mandates are found in both Testaments. Do you ever wonder what God may think of Bible-waving Christians who don't know the Bible has an Old Testament in it? Some of us may not really care whether something is in the Bible.

Well, let me take time to point out that in the two mandates we have two "Thus says the Lord." And we have both of them in the law and in the gospels of the canon of Scripture. Do not fail to tie the cultural mandate of Genesis 1 with the Great Commandment of Matthew 22. As to the evangelistic mandate of Matthew 28, I find an Old Testament antecedant for it in Genesis 3 where the Lord called out to Adam, "Where are you?" (v. 9). There is a world of truth in verse 15 where God says of the seed of the woman, "he shall bruise your head," and to the serpent, "and you shall bruise his heel." It is with good reason that we call that verse the *proto evangelion* (or the original gospel).

The good news is that the woman's seed will bruise the head of the serpent. In other words, he will deal a death blow to the serpent. Based on Genesis 3:15, we may say that evangelism is bruising the head of the serpent. It is killing the devil; it is destroying evil; it is ridding the world of the powers of darkness and evil.

Other Old Testament References

Canon Stanley G. Evans summarizes the Old Testament's social position in five points:
- The service of God is ethical before it is ceremonial.
- God is concerned with corporate morality.
- A first moral duty is the demand of justice for the poor.
- The purpose of God is national perfection.
- There will be no national perfection, or even national survival, while the people forsake the ways of God.[5]

Moses was God's liberator as well as His lawgiver. Moses thundered out to Pharaoh, "Let my people go" (Ex. 5:1). *Exodus* literally means "the road out."

God is the God of justice. He says through His fiery prophet Amos: "let justice roll down like waters, and righteousness like an ever-flowing stream" (5:24). Justice is not the same thing as charity or compassion or mercy or benevolence. What God requires is justice. Only justice clothes persons with dignity, and God wants justice to flow like a mighty river, not just to trickle down a few drops at a time.

Where did Paul get that famous text of his, "The just shall live by faith"? He took it, of course, from the prophet Habakkuk (see Hab. 2:4 and Rom. 1:17, esp. in the King James Version). To the Hebrews, persons are what they do. If they do righteousness, they are righteous. The just live by faith because faith is something you do daily.[6]

Isaiah 61:1-2 became the text for our Lord's inaugural sermon in His hometown of Nazareth (see Luke 4:16-30). Does not that text uniquely combine the cultural and evangelistic mandates? Good tidings are proclaimed, and good deeds are performed.

The "year of the Lord's favor" (Isa. 61:2) is the year of Jubilee, every fiftieth year. Through the year of Jubilee, the Hebrews sought to raise a bulwark against slavery and many other social evils. The year of Jubilee and the sabbath year called the Jews back to an acknowledgment that the land belonged to God and not to them. It reminded the Hebrews that a prior social mortgage exists on all property.

The message of the Hebrew prophets is that ritual and emotional religion is harmful unless it results in righteousness. The prophets admirably wedded human freedom and responsibility. G. K. Chesterton spoke of an anarchist who claimed that since freedom was an inalienable human right, he had a right to punch someone on the nose. Chesterton replied: "No. Your freedom ends where my nose begins." That was the message of the prophets.

Some churches which talk about "the full gospel" offer only the priestly half of the gospel. They neglect the prophetic half of the good news. The church exercising her prophetic ministry can help her members and the world think Christianly about controversial questions.

The God of the eighth-century prophets of Israel is still calling us to say and do something about the social blight all around us. The God of Amos, Isaiah, and Micah is our God and guide also.

Who will be a voice for the voiceless? Is that not a proper role for the church? What about the Christian prophet to whom the word of the Lord comes? Shall the prophet not speak for those who cannot speak for themselves?

The Healing Ministry of Jesus

There is also a strong biblical connection between evangelism and Christian social involvement in the healing ministry of Jesus. Some Christians are hesitant about connecting evangelism with physical healings and exorcisms. But the two were certainly together in our Lord's healing ministry.

The case of Legion in Mark 5:1-20 is one example which may be cited. The artificial distinction which we so readily make between soul winning and social involvement is shot to smithereens in that case. Legion, or the Gerasene demoniac as you may prefer to call him, was naked and out of his right mind. He was enslaved to the powers of darkness and evil. Jesus ministered to all of Legion's needs—physical, psychological, social, and spiritual. The end result of it all was that Legion was sent back home to bear witness to how much the Lord had done for him.

The case of the paralytic carried by four friends to Jesus is a second example which shows the interfacing of evangelism and Christian social involvement in the healing ministry of Jesus (see Mark 2:1-12). The first thing Jesus said to the paralytic was, "My son your sins are forgiven" (v. 5). However, the last thing He said to him was, "Rise, take up your pallet and go home" (v. 11) First, in this case, our Lord dealt with the sin problem. Then, He dealt with the physical problem.

However, the opposite order is seen in the case of a man blind from birth whom Jesus healed (John 9). The man was sent to the pool of Siloam. Later, Jesus dealt with his faith problem (see vv. 1-41).

A final case which may be cited to show this interfacing of evangelism and Christian social involvement in the healing ministry of Jesus is the case of the official whose son was ill (John 4:46-54). After the man's son was healed, the Scripture says: "He himself believed, and all his household" (v. 53).

These healing miracles in John's Gospel are recited for evangelistic purposes. According to the writer of the Fourth Gospel, Jesus did other signs, "but these are written that you may believe that Jesus is the Christ, the Son of God, and that believing you may have life in his name" (John 20:31).

The Mission of Jesus

A fourth biblical connection between evangelism and Christian social ministries may be seen in the mission of Jesus as stated in Luke 4:18-19. If you haven't been "Luke foured" to death, please look at that passage one more time:

> The Spirit of the Lord is upon me,
> because he has anointed me to
>   preach good news to the poor.
> He has sent me to proclaim release
>   to the captives
>   and recovering of sight to the blind,
>   to set at liberty those who are oppressed,
>   to proclaim the acceptable year of the
>   Lord.

It is truly hard to tell where evangelism and Christian social involvement begin and end in that passage, isn't it? "We don't see here a theology that divides a man up into little compartments—body, mind, soul, emotions, spirit—then puts one above the other and deals with that only."[7]

The union of religion and ethics "reached its highest perfection in the life and mind of Jesus," said Walter Rauschenbusch. Notice how Jesus, in this inaugural sermon, described His work in terms of preaching, healing, and releasing prisoners.

Substantial evidence has been marshalled to show that this message was a call to observe Jubilee. Jesus interpreted His role in social terms. His targets were the poor, the captives, the blind, and the oppressed. Jesus saw Himself as God's instrument for human liberation.

For the poor and oppressed of the world, there need be no demythologization of those words from Luke 4. In fact, if the words are demythologized, they lose their cutting edge for the poor and oppressed.

The Rich Man and Lazarus

A fifth biblical connection between evangelism and Christian social involvement may be seen in the story about the rich man and Lazarus (see Luke 16:19-31). Lazarus had been in dire need of some social ministries. The five brothers of the rich man were in need of escaping the place of torment to which their brother had gone. But the solemn word from Father Abraham, who represents God in the story, is: "If they do not hear Moses and the prophets, neither will they be convinced if some one should rise from the dead" (v. 31).

Appropriate social ministry was not rendered to Lazarus because the rich man refused to hear and head the Law and the Prophets. The five brothers of Dives could not be evangelized unless they would hear and heed the Law and the Prophets. Neither Christian social involvement nor evangelism will occur unless persons hear and heed the Word of God.

I would remind you that our Lord Himself summarized the Law and the Prophets in terms of loving God supremely and neighbor as self. Only our obedience to that word of the Lord will result in balanced evangelism and symmetrical Christian social involvement.

The Judgment of the Nations

Still a sixth biblical connection between evangelism and Christian social ministries may be seen in the judgment of the nations' scene, recorded in Matthew 25:31-46. Evangelists warn persons of the judgment of God. And well they might, for just as certainly as we live and die, we shall all be judged by God.

There are several surprises, however, in this judgment scene of Matthew 25. The nations, and not merely individuals, are judged here. Moreover, this judgment is on the basis of deeds and not of words: "As you did it to one of the least of these my brethren, you did it to me" (v. 40). Furthermore, both those who did and did not do the deeds mentioned were surprised. Finally, the fact that "the least of these" were Christ's brethren was a surprise.

Today hunger stalks many parts of the earth like a hungry lion. Perhaps as many as thirty thousand children die daily of starvation. More persons have been killed from starvation in the last five years than from all of the wars, revolutions, and murders of the last century. Every day up to forty thousand persons die of hunger, thirty thousand of whom are children.[8] Doesn't Matthew 25:45 shed some light on our obligation to "the least of these"?

If we are unwilling to share with others those things which do not last, how shall we share that which is everlasting? A Presbyterian pastor preached a sermon in 1982 entitled, "Being Neighbor in Deed to Neighbors in Need," based on Matthew 25:31-46. One paragraph in the sermon went like this:

> The criterion by which we shall be judged will not be questions such as who can recite the Apostles' Creed. It will not be did you invite Jesus into your heart at the last revival. ... Instead it will be just one question: Did you care enough to be a neighbor in deed to your neighbor in need?"[9]

How do you respond to those words?

I can tell you this. The Christian faith is more than mere talk. The kind of disciple Christ wants is the one whose walk will match his or her talk and whose talk will match his or her walk. Evangelization or social involvement which does not endeavor to produce that kind of disciple may be offering cheap grace to the perishing. I fear that if we and our converts do not give food to the hungry, drink to the thirsty, welcome to strangers, clothes to the naked, and make visits to the sick and the prisoners, we shall be numbered with the stinking goats and be sent away into eternal punishment. If we can't find a word from the Lord in Matthew 25 about feeding the undernourished, caring for the sick, rehabilitating prisoners, clothing the destitute, and housing refugees, we may be both blind and deaf spiritually.

Other New Testament Passages

There are, of course, many other Scriptures which point to this connecting of evangelism and social involvement.

Sometimes Scriptures which we overlook and downplay say as much or more about us than those passages which we lift up and to which we pay so much attention. Take Ephesians 2:8-9 for example. We like to preach salvation by grace through faith plus nothing else. But often we overlook Ephesians 2:10 which tells us that we are God's work of art "created in Christ Jesus for good works." Another example is Ephesians 4:28 which reads: "Let the thief no longer steal, but rather let him labor, doing honest work with his hands, so that he may be able to give to those in need."

The Magnificat of Mary in Luke 1:46-55 is a strong passage which shows the social conscience of Mary, the mother of Jesus. Sherwood Eliot Wirt points out that "the time is overdue for a fresh appraisal of Mary's social conscience." Wirt ties Mary's influence to John the Baptist, to James the brother of our Lord, and to Luke the physician.[10]

Mary sang as though the future had become the past. These words came from the Galilean peasant girl who became the mother of our Lord. They are chanted daily in churches around the world. See how they deal with the traditional enemies of humankind. Someone has called the Magnificat a battle hymn of democracy. Most likely it should be tied to the song of Hannah in 1 Samuel 2:1-10.

John the Baptist also had a social conscience. Did his older cousin, Mary, influence him? When John said: "Be content with your wages," he meant "stop bullying and extorting from the citizenry of Palestine. Let the troops live within their incomes and stop milking the countryside."[11]

That reference to a saying of John the Baptist comes from Luke 3:14. So much of the rich material on social involvement comes from Luke, the physician. Renan once called the Gospel of Luke "the most beautiful book in the world." Why? Primarily because of the social compassion that permeates the text.

Furthermore, have you ever meditated on what is "pure and undefiled" religion according to James 1:26-27? It is religion which bridles the tongue, visits orphans and widows in their affliction, and keeps oneself unstained from the world.

Biblical Origins

Have we fully grasped what Jesus meant when He said the sabbath was made for persons and not persons for the sabbath (see Mark 2:27)? It does mean He was an iconoclast who broke some of the sacred traditions of the elders. But it also means He was placing persons above social and religious institutions.

Conclusion

Jesus was "a prophet mighty in deed and word before God and all the people" (Luke 24:19). If He is our model, we too shall endeavor to be mighty in deed and word.

Notes

1. Cited by Gustavo Gutierrez in "A Spirituality for Liberation," *The Other Side*, vol. 21, no. 3, issue 162, April/May, 1985, p. 42.

2. The Reformed Ecumenical Synod in its *Testimony on Human Rights* identified Genesis 1:26-31 and Psalm 8 with the cultural mandate. See Paul G. Schrotenboer, "Testimony on Human Rights, The Reformed Ecumenical Synod: A Precis," *Transformation*, vol. 1, no. 3, July-September, 1984, p. 13. I recommend that readers who are interested in pursuing the two mandates further, read C. Peter Wagner, *Church Growth and the Whole Gospel: A Biblical Mandate* (San Francisco: Harper & Row, Publishers, 1981), pp. 1-68.

3. See John Stott, "The Great Commandment . . . The Great Commission," *World Evangelization*, Information Bulletin No. 23, June, 1981, p. 5.

4. John Perkins, *A Quiet Revolution* (Waco, Texas: Word Books, Publisher, 1976), p. 3.

5. See Stanley G. Evans, *The Social Hope of the Church* (London: Hodder & Stoughton, 1965), p. 19.

6. I do not intend to imply here that persons are saved by their works.

7. Perkins, p. 65.

8. Cited in "World Hunger Update," *Light*, May-June, 1982, p. 12.

9. Cited by John Robinson, "Care Shown for Neighbors in Need Stressed as Criterion for Christian," *The News and Observer*, Raleigh, N. C., July 19, 1982, p. 1C.

10. See Sherwood Eliot Wirt, *The Social Conscience of the Evangelical* (New York: Harper & Row, Publishers, 1968), pp. 14-15.

11. Ibid., p. 14.

3
Historical Roots

Scripture Lesson: Joel 2:28-29; Philemon 4-22

Evangelism and social involvement are analagous to the two ears of a person. If we hear only with one ear, our hearing is impaired.

I have selected for this chapter a few historical examples which may help us to see how the church has heard with both ears. Admittedly, the examples are incomplete and quite skimpy. They are more like paradigms or even vignettes in places. Nevertheless, they may put us in touch with some historical roots of our faith which can improve our hearing.

These examples reveal that the church, like individual Christians, has sometimes had hearing problems with both ears. The social involvement ear tends toward social service rather than social action.

As we look back over nearly twenty centuries of church history, perhaps the best we can say about the church is that it never quite forgot Jesus Christ. The worst we can say about the church is that it often ignored what He said and did.

I know that the pages of church history are smeared with every sin known to humankind. Christians committed to the highest principles have in the name of those very principles violated them. I wish to condemn all such villainies and to condone none of them. Therefore, I freely admit that the examples I have chosen are very selective. Nevertheless, they are true, and to some extent they are also representative.

The Early Church

Almost everybody would agree that the early church was evangelistic, but what about social involvement? Churches living at the margins of a society will exercise a different role than those living at the centers of a culture. How did the early church combine evangelism and social involvement?

She combined the two in her confession, "Jesus is Lord" (1 Cor. 12:3; see Phil. 2:11). That earliest creed of the church was the quintessence of the gospel message which the church proclaimed, but it was also a political term. I do not mean to imply that the early Christians were political agitators or even that they had a self-conscious social ethic. But they were political enough to remember that politicians had executed Jesus. As the Apostles' Creed said of Him, he was "crucified under Pontius Pilate." Also the term *Lord,* which came from their belief in Christ's resurrection, advertised Christ's dominion over all other lordships, including that of the Romans.

Every time the followers of Christ gathered for worship and made that confession, the Romans who wanted to conquer the world and who insisted that Caesar was lord felt threatened. It wasn't that the Romans were against religion or wanted all people to accept the Roman culture. All they asked for was that religion do its share to make law-abiding Roman citizens—a very modest share like saluting the flag of Rome once a year and burning a pinch of incense before the bust of Caesar in the town square.

Perhaps you are thinking, *That doesn't sound like such a big request.* Why then did the Christians go to the lions? The answer is over that single radical question of lordship. Donald W. Shriver, Jr. comments:

> It was the one point in their articles of faith that was inherently political. It was more political than some of their own theologians knew; more political . . . than Paul himself knew when he was writing the 13th chapter of Romans; more mundanely political, even, than the author of Revelation 13 knew as he envisioned the great eschatological comeuppance reserved by the God of Jesus for the empires of this world. Little did John of Patmos imagine that less than three centuries later the churches of the empire would have held out so long against the lordly pretensions of emperors that an em-

peror would make peace with the church by abandoning his claim to lordship; or that in this action the Gospel of the Resurrection would be structuring a change in the relations of religion and the state that reverberated through the next thousand years of medieval Christendom, with enough left over to help shape new political systems in yet the next 400 years too.[1]

Somewhere I read that there is a cemetery in Palestine, Texas, which has a tombstone with an unusual inscription. Following the name of the man, was inscribed: "December 13, 1853-December 19, 1927. He loved relatives, friends and country; was fond of games and sports; believed in God and Christianity, but denounced Political Preachers." However sympathetic we may feel with that brother, the plain truth is that whoever confesses, "Jesus Christ is Lord," is necessarily political to the extent that he or she has already delegitimated all other totalitarian claims of power. This is as true today as it was in the first Christian century.

A second way in which the early church put evangelism and social involvement together was in her own internal fellowship. The church's gospel transformed the internal life of the church into an inclusive fellowship. An inclusive church was a consequence and sign of her proclamation that Jesus is Lord. Hellenistic Jews were brought into the church along with Palestinian Jews on the day of Pentecost (see Acts 2 and 6). The eunuch from Ethiopia became a Christian (Acts 8). Samaritans were brought in (Acts 8). Cornelius, a Roman centurion, and his Gentile household were added to the faith (Acts 10 and 11). An evangelistic mission was launched to the Gentiles (Acts 13:44-52). A conference at the mother church in Jerusalem concluded that Gentiles did not have to be circumcised in order to become Christians (Acts 15). The Acts of the Apostles closes with Paul in Rome, the capital of the Roman empire, "preaching the kingdom of God and teaching about the Lord Jesus Christ quite openly and unhindered" (28:31).

The Epistles of the New Testament tell the same story of inclusiveness that we read in Acts. That prophecy of Joel 2 was being fulfilled in the church (see Acts 2:16-21). God poured out His Spirit upon all—Jews and Gentiles, men and women, young and old. Those who were far off were brought near in the blood of Christ: "For he is our peace, who has made us both one, and has broken down the dividing wall of hostility . . . that he might create in himself one new man in place of the two" (Eph. 2:14-15).

Slavery abounded in the Roman Empire, but converted slaves were considered brothers and sisters in the early church. Paul led Onesimus, a runaway slave, to Christ; but Paul sent Onesimus back to Philemon, his owner, calling him "no longer a slave but more than a slave, . . . a beloved brother . . . both in the flesh and in the Lord" (Philem. 16). Right there the gospel ax was laid against the roots of slavery.

The same apostle who evangelized Onesimus declared: "There is neither Jew nor Greek, there is neither slave nor free, there is neither male nor female; for you are all one in Christ Jesus" (Gal. 3:28). I do not wonder that James Russell Lowell said, "There is dynamite enough in the New Testament, if illegitimately applied, to blow all our existing institutions to atoms."[2] The gospel is in some respects like a time bomb. It becomes social dynamite when given time to work.

You will note that I have so far said nothing in this account of the early church about persons like Tabitha of Joppa who was "full of good works and acts of charity" (Acts 9:36). I have concentrated on the church's message, "Jesus is Lord," and on the way that gospel was transformative inside the church. We might even say that the early church was herself a part of the gospel promise and not simply a result of gospel promise. Since that is true, the early church was herself a form of evangelism as Shriver has convincingly argued.[3]

Beyond all of that, we may point to the merging of evangelism and social involvement (especially in the form of social ministry) in a number of New Testament passages. A striking example is the healing of Aeneas in Acts 9. Aeneas, who had been bedridden for eight years and was paralyzed, heard Peter say to him: "Aeneas, Jesus Christ heals you; rise and make your bed" (v. 34). But where was the evangelism? "And all the residents of Lydda and Sharon saw him, and they turned to the Lord" (v. 35).

Take the lame beggar at the gate of the Temple in Acts 3 as another example. People had to carry the man about. He had been lame from birth. Peter told him, "I have no silver and gold, but I give you what I have; in the name of Jesus Christ of Nazareth, walk" (v. 6). What a marvelous sight that must have been! Where was the evangelism to accompany the social service of healing? A crowd assembled quickly. Peter began: "Men of Israel, why do you wonder at this, or why do you stare at us, as though by our own power or piety we had made him walk?" (v. 12). That was the occasion for a sermon in which Peter called the people to repent of their sins and turn to the One who had healed the lame man.

I am sure we could find other examples, but don't overlook that of the seven in Acts 6. When the seven were appointed to serve tables, Luke summarized: "And the word of God increased; and the number of disciples multiplied greatly in Jerusalem, and a great many of the priests were obedient to the faith" (v. 7). In that instance, an internal act of service to Hellenist widows was coupled with a powerful evangelistic thrust. It should not escape our attention that the only person whom the New Testament calls "the evangelist" was Philip, one of the seven (Acts 21:8). That same Philip took the gospel to Samaria and to the Ethiopian eunuch (Acts 8).

There is no way we can escape the fact that, in the early church, the disciples followed in the footsteps of our Lord. They shared the good news as He did. They served others like He had done; and they even suffered as He had.

Modern Missions

Sherwood Eliot Wirt concluded that "the Christian social conscience found its most creative expression . . . in the missionary movement that carried the Gospel around the world."[4] The modern missionary movement, going back nearly two centuries has frequently connected evangelism

Historical Roots

and social involvement, and especially so in regard to social service.

September 20, 1984 marked the one hundreth anniversary of the Protestant church in Korea. God used a medical missionary by the name of Horace Allen to open the door to Protestant missionaries in Korea. Dr. Allen had previously been a medical missionary to China. He began his work as the appointed physician to the American delegation in Seoul.

On December 4, 1884 a plot against Korea's leaders exploded into violence. Many of the king's counselors were murdered. The queen's nephew lay dying in a pool of blood. Slashed with seven sword cuts in the head and body, fourteen palace physicians were about to pour black pitch into his wounds. Over their objection Dr. Allen was called in to save the prince's life. For three months, it was nip and tuck as Dr. Allen fought to restore the prince to health. A grateful king appointed Dr. Allen as physician to the royal court and permitted him to open a hospital in Seoul, sponsored by the government and "a benevolent society in America." That was the first official approval by the Korean government of missionary work in Korea. Dr. Allen became the first resident Protestant missionary.[5]

The church may be growing faster in South Korea than in any other country of the world. Reasons for that rapid growth are complex and multiple, but would there be a growth strong enough to tell about apart from the pioneering work of Horace Allen who in his own life and ministry beautifully wedded evangelism and social involvement?

Others continue to build upon Allen's foundations. George Hays, area director for Southern Baptist missionaries in East Asia reported to his Foreign Mission Board on the 1984 work of Wallace Memorial Hospital in Korea:

> Decisions for Christ were made by 2,028 patients out of a total number of 43,386 non-believers who received a Christian witness through the hospital. Free care was given to 3,814 persons with a total dollar value of $306,948. One hundred and two hospital personnel were involved in a total of

21 medical/evangelistic trips of the mobile clinic. Eighteen professions of faith were made in 14 evangelistic services held at these clinics.[6]

Most denominations and some of the faith-type mission boards have been, and continue to be, involved in medical care; although in the last quarter of this century, D. A. McGavran and others in the Church Growth Movement have raised some questions about all kinds of institutional missions except that which multiplies local churches. Southern Baptists, for example, continue unapologetically to combine the meeting of spiritual and physical needs.

Medical doctor Franklin Fowler, who retired in 1985 as senior medical consultant for the Southern Baptist Foreign Mission Board, had a wholistic view of mission work which coupled health care ministries with evangelism. One of Fowler's major contributions in thirty-seven years of missionary service was a continuing emphasis on the evangelistic ministry of health care workers. Fowler helped found the first Baptist hospital in Paraguay. The hospital was located in Asuncion largely because of that city's evangelistic potential. All roads in Paraguay lead to Asuncion.[7]

A Baptist Medical-Dental Fellowship was begun in 1977. The organization's 1,280 plus members provide mission support and disaster relief as they work in cooperation with the Southern Baptist Convention's (SBC) Home and Foreign Mission Boards, the Brotherhood Commission, and Woman's Missionary Union. Composed of physicians, dentists, and medical and dental students, this spiritually oriented professional organization supports medical missions around the world. In 1983, 157 medical/dental volunteers served the Foreign Mission Board as short-term volunteers. Other members provided funds for continuing medical education for career missionaries and scholarships for the children of missionaries attending medical or dental school.

The fellowship seeks to complement the work already being done by the agricultural, evangelistic, and other missionaries in a ministry to the whole person. Two facts help motivate its members to extend the healing ministry of

Historical Roots

Christ around the world. According to Henry Lane, executive director of the fellowship, 52 percent of the world has never seen a doctor or received any kind of medical treatment. Furthermore, one-third of Christ's ministry was spent in healing the sick.[8]

The missionary concern for meeting a broad range of human needs can also be seen outside the denominational mission boards. I have been personally blessed and inspired by the life and ministry of the late Cameron Townsend. Townsend founded the Wycliffe Bible Translators. When he died at the age of eighty-five, his organization comprised a staff of over 4,200, scattered across the globe. His mission was to translate the Bible into every spoken language.

It all seemed to crystalize for Townsend when a Cakchiquel Indian in Guatemala asked him, "If your God is so smart, why doesn't he speak Cakchiquel?" After twelve years of arduous labor, Townsend had translated the New Testament into Cakchiquel and presented the first published book in that language to the president of Guatemala.

Along the way in his spare time, Townsend had founded five schools, a clinic, a printing press, an orphanage, and a coffee cooperative. Churches sprang up. Arcane customs of witchcraft gradually disappeared.

Townsend also discovered that 5,171 languages are known to exist today. The Bible had been translated into only sixty-seven languages at the beginning of the twentieth century. Now, portions of it are in 1,700 languages. Translation work progresses in another 1,200. Linguists are tackling a new language every thirteen days. The man called affectionately "Uncle Cam" had much to do with making it possible for every person to read the Bible in his or her own language.[9]

I do not mean to imply that all missions and/or missionaries have been in agreement on emphasizing a ministry to the whole person. Take the case of missionary James Endicott for instance. At one point in 1980, the best-seller list in Canada carried a biography of Endicott. He was a Canadian missionary to China during the 1920s and 1930s but was ostracized by his church and by most people in his native country when he stormily resigned from his missionary post.

Endicott resigned because he was dismayed over the way Western missionaries seemingly ignored the suffering of the millions of Chinese peasants who were dying of horrible starvation directly caused by political interests. He felt that he could no longer associate with missionaries who deemphasized preaching and social service, which they said stirred up young Christians and admonished them to agitate about the conditions of the masses.

Here was a missionary who saw that for his time in China a word from the Lord could come only from a strong sense of God's immanence. Endicott sensed the need to recognize how utterly serious God is about human needs and world affairs. He believed that we are required to make concrete choices about how we respond to such overwhelming needs. It is a bit ironic that only forty years later the Canadian churches were beginning to see that Endicott made a strong point when he claimed that Jesus never emphasized creed and liturgy over behavior.[10]

The issues raised by Endicott and his kind have not all been settled yet. Professor Paul Hiebert of Fuller Theological Seminary's School of World Mission has expressed the opinion that "it will be increasingly difficult to carry out our commission in countries abroad unless we are willing to deal with the full range of human needs including health and development." He thinks the dichotomy we make between ministry to human needs and spiritual needs is a result of the introduction of Greek thought into the church through the conversion of Gentiles. "We need a new integrated theology," contends Hiebert, "that rejects the platonic dichotomy we have inherited from Aquinas and others." What Hiebert argues for is evangelism through education, hospitals, preaching, personal witnessing, and so on. Our problem is that we don't see *all* of these as spiritual tasks. Hospitals and schools should not be seen as secondary functions in the Christian world mission, according to Hiebert.[11]

Stan Rowland, a health coordinator with Life Ministry

Uganda (Campus Crusade for Christ), contends that both spiritual and vocational multiplication can take place through community health evangelists. These are trained part-time volunteers who view medical care as "a servant to the spiritual ministry." One such community health evangelism (CHE) training project began in Buhugu, Uganda, in May of 1982. It is a joint project of the Church of Uganda, Mission Moving Mountains, Life Ministry, and the local government. Twelve CHE volunteers from ten villages around Buhugu were trained three days a week for ten weeks. So far, over four hundred persons have confessed Christ as Lord and Savior, and each volunteer has up to three follow-up groups of ten to fifteen persons.[12]

The Clapham Sect

The Clapham Sect was an evangelical group of aristocratic politicians, bankers, and Anglican clerics of Clapham and Cambridge who worked for reform from within the church establishment. They frequently gathered in the home of William Wilberforce, one of their leaders who lived in a suburb of London known as Clapham. That's how these evangelical philanthropists became known as the Clapham Sect. They were not a formal religious party. All of them were members of the Church of England, though they were frequently denounced by High Anglican Tories as Methodists.

These men were products of the evangelical awakenings in both England and America. Particularly were they indebted to the earlier work of John Wesley and George Whitefield. Though they were connected with the establishment, their primary business was with personal salvation and moral reforms with individuals as opposed to corporate religion. Mostly they were a group of Christian laymen in the London area dedicated to applying Christian principles in public life.[13]

Two of the most prominent members of the Clapham Sect were William Wilberforce (1759-1833) and the seventh Lord Shaftesbury, Anthony Ashley Cooper (1801-1885). Consider briefly the work of these two men.

Wilberforce's conversion began in 1785 with a reading of Philip Doddridge's book, *On the Rise and Progress of Religion in the Soul.* Later Wilberforce and his cousin, Isaac Milner, spent hours reading and discussing the New Testament. His conversion two hundred years ago profoundly altered the lives of multitudes of persons whom he never saw because he was largely responsible for the abolition of slavery in the British empire.

When converted, Wilberforce was already a member of Parliament. His intention was to become a vocational Christian minister. John Newton, the evangelical hymn writer and former slave captain, persuaded him instead to serve the Lord in the House of Commons. Wilberforce determined to champion the cause of abolishing the slave traffic and slavery itself. John Wesley, three days prior to his own death, wrote a letter of encouragement to Wilberforce. Wesley, in that brief letter of only one paragraph, called slavery "that execrable villiany which is the scandal of religion, of England, and of human nature."[14]

Roland H. Bainton of Yale used the story of Wilberforce and William Pitt (1759-1806) to illustrate how pastors with their God-given commitment to conservation and prophets with their God-given commitment to innovation can collaborate for the common good.

Pitt served as prime minister in England and Wilberforce served as a member of Parliament. They were good friends even though the friendship suffered strain through Wilberforce's unrelenting opposition to slavery which he wanted to focus on in every session of Parliament but which Pitt resisted lest opposition to antislavery harden to the detriment of both the slaves and the society. Wilberforce kept hammering away against slavery, and Pitt kept inching Parliament along until, after thirty years, the *slave trade* was abolished. So the pressure was continued for another twenty years until finally, on the day before Wilberforce died, Parliament voted the money to indemnify the slaveholders and free some 800,000 slaves throughout all the British dominions. Pitt and Wilberforce today are buried in Westminster Abbey, side by side.[15]

Lord Shaftesbury, another member of the Clapham Sect, did much to Christianize the socioeconomic structures of Great Britain in the nineteenth century. He attacked the chimney-sweep scandal, child labor in factories, female labor in mines, the overlong working hours, lack of safety and medical protection, and the unhealthy working conditions.[16]

The Second Great Awakening

America has experienced three and possibly four great spiritual awakenings. Those awakenings have been accompanied and spread through revivalism. Wherever genuine revival occurs you can usually find evangelism in blue-hot heat. Can we say the same thing though for social involvement?

The name of Charles Grandison Finney (1792-1875) is almost synonymous with the Second Great Awakening. Finney reigned supreme as the dean of itinerant evangelists in America for fifty years (1825-1875). He introduced new measures into revivals, such as holding protracted meetings in cities for four consecutive days and nights, calling penitents to make an immediate decision to come forward in the service during the public invitation to an inquiry room for counseling, and letting women pray publicly in mixed gatherings. "It is difficult but necessary for modern students to realize ... that in the nineteenth century revival measures, being new, usually went hand in hand with progressive theology and humanitarian concern."[17]

Finney may have been the foremost promoter of revivals and social reformation in the nineteenth century. "Revivals are hindered," wrote Finney in his 1835 *Lectures on Revivals of Religion*, "when ministers and churches take wrong ground in regard to any question involving human rights."[18] He argued in his *Lectures on Systematic Theology* that the spirit of the Christian is "necessarily that of the reformer. To the reformation of the world they stand committed."[19]

In one of his letters on revival in the *Oberlin Evangelist*, this last of the outstanding itinerant evangelists to espouse postmillenialism, asserted that "the great business of the church is to reform the world—to put away every kind of sin." He went on in that same place to say, "The church of Christ was originally organized to be a body of reformers."[20] This evangelist who led so many hundreds to Christ saw the reformation of humankind as the "appropriate" work of the church. He wanted to see the church as a body, and not just as individual Christians, involved in such moral reforms as the abolition of slavery, prohibition, and the eradication of prostitution.

As late as 1868, Finney insisted that the loss of interest in benevolent enterprises was usually evidence of a "blackslidden heart." Among the benevolent works, he specified good government, Christian education, temperance reform, the abolition of slavery, and relief of the poor.[21]

Long before the advent of liberation theology, Finney recognized that God has a preference for the poor, not because He is prejudiced but because He is the God of justice. Finney insisted on a system of free pews in churches. In Finney's day, many churches used pew rentals to raise construction and maintenance costs. Prices actually varied like in a theater where the best seats cost the most.

A practical result of pew rental was often that church seating reflected social and economic class. The poor were relegated either to the few, rugged, free pews in the balcony or in the back of the church house; or, more tragic still, they were altogether excluded from the churches. Finney and his friends found this abominable system of church financing a direct contradiction to a gospel freely offered to all. They built "Free Churches" open to all. For example, Finneyite Free Churches became a distinct branch of New York Presbyterianism, where they grouped themselves into a special Third Presbytery. Some evidence exists that these churches were the great centers of reform in the nineteenth century.[22]

So impressive were Finney's efforts that Harry F. Ward, an advocate of social evangelism, wrote in 1915:

> The mighty evangelism of the middle of the last century

created as one of its by-products the moral standards of the formative community life of the Middle West. It turned licentious, drunken, brawling people into folks who began to organize their communities on the basis of purity, temperance, and a decent respect for the rights and opinions of others.[23]

"Finney speaks to us today," said Professor Timothy Smith of Johns Hopkins University, "because he recognized the personal character of the spirituality that unites individual with social salvation." This champion of all kinds of reforms, from his earliest days to his last breath, continued Smith, "insisted that the primary task of those who would change the world must ever remain in the conversion of sinners through preaching the gospel in the power of the Holy Spirit."[24]

The Confessing Church of Germany

Run these images through your mind: shaved heads, sunken eyes, piled-up corpses, black smoke from the crematoria, a sickening sweet odor that once you have smelled you can never forget. Surely those images bring to our minds the Holocaust, that horrible extinction of between eleven and twelve million persons by Hitler—6 million of them Jews, and many of whom were women and children.

Against the background of such unprecedented corporate evil, the Confessing Church of Germany was formed. Many Christians celebrated in 1984 the fiftieth anniversary of the Confessing Church, which Dietrich Bonhoeffer and others launched in 1934 with a church synod at the Westphalian town of Barmen about seventeen miles west of Dusseldorf. Those who drew up the famous Barmen Declaration intended to resist the Nazis' largely successful efforts to turn the church into a tool of state power and German nationalism.

John Godsey, one of Bonhoeffer's biographers said: "He saw it was the duty of the church not just to bind the wounds of those hit by a madman driving down the boulevard but to put a stick in the spokes of his wheel and stop the driver." That statement in no wise is intended to depict Bonhoeffer as anything less than a devout Christian. "He was one of the very few persons I have ever met for whom God was real and always near," said Payne Best, an English officer and fellow prisoner with him in the SS prison at Flossenburg, Germany.

Bonhoeffer was hanged on April 9, 1945, along with five other persons implicated in the conspiracy to assassinate Adolf Hitler in July 1944. His friends called him "one of the first guilty martyrs." He accepted guilt for the Nazi crimes "on behalf of all German people."[25]

Martin Niemoeller became a navy cadet at eighteen. By the end of World War I, he had become commander of a U-boat. In 1934 he, too, assisted with the formation of the Confessing Church in Germany. The Confessing Church claimed sole authority as the Protestant church of Jesus Christ in Germany. Its theology was one of the cross rather than Germanic superiority.[26]

Niemoeller was arrested by Hitler in 1937 and did not get out of prison until the end of World War II. In a sermon preached not long after his eight-year imprisonment was over, Pastor Niemoeller said:

> We have no right to pass off all guilt on the evil Nazis. ... We have done little to stop the corruption and, above all, we the church failed. For we knew which way was false and which right, yet let people run unwarned into ruination. I do not exclude myself from this guilt, for I too have kept silent when I should have spoken.[27]

Surely one lesson of Barmen is that there is a time and place when Christians are not only entitled but obligated to resist criminal governments and to resist immoral actions by legitimate governments. Another lesson is that corporate sin produces corporate guilt, and corporate guilt needs to be confessed. We see also in the Confessing Church evangelization through suffering and martydom.

Historical Roots

Notes

1. Donald W. Shriver, Jr., "Gospel Message and Social Witness; The Church as a Form of Evangelism," *Perkins Journal,* vol. XXXV, no. 1, Fall, 1981, p. 6.
2. Quoted by Walter Rauschenbusch, *Christianity and the Social Crisis* (New York George H. Doran Co., 1907), p. 89.
3. Shriver, pp. 3-11.
4. Sherwood Eliot Wirt, *The Social Conscience of the Evangelical* (New York: Harper & Row, Publishers, 1968), pp. 32-33.
5. Based on Samuel Hugh Moffett, "Korea's Unconquerable Christians," *Decision,* vol. 25, no. 7-8, July-August, 1984, p. 7.
6. Report to the Foreign Mission Board, Feb. 13, 1985, p. 5.
7. Mary Jane Welch, "Medical Pioneer Looks Back: 'Starting Things' His Specialty," *Religious Herald,* vol. CLVIII, no. 11, March 14, 1985, pp. 14-15.
8. Brenda J. Sanders, " 'Help Wanted' Offers Mission Opportunities," *Word and Way,* vol. 12, no. 13, March 29, 1984, p. 9.
9. Philip Yancey, "Cam Townsend's Mission: Let God Do the Talking," *Christianity Today,* vol. XXVI, no. 11, June 18, 1982, pp. 14-18.
10. The previous three paragraphs are based on an Advent meditation by Bonnie Greene in *Sojourners,* vol. 9, no. 12, December 1980, p. 27.
11. See Paul Hiebert's guest editorial, "Mission's Devastating Dichotomy," *Global Church Growth,* vol. XIX, no. 6, November-December 1982, p. 224.
12. Stan Rowland, "Training Local Villagers to Provide Health Care," *Evangelical Missions Quarterly,* vol. 21, no. 1, January 1985, pp. 44-50.
13. See Rebecca J. Winter, *The Night Cometh: Two Wealthy Evangelicals Face the Nations* (South Pasadena, Calif.: William Carey Library, 1977), p. 29.
14. See Wirt, pp. 35-36. Also, see Leslie K. Tarr, "The Great Change: The Story of William Wilberforce's Conversion 200 Years Ago," *Decision,* vol. 26, no. 2, February 1985, pp. 14-15.
15. Related by Foy Valentine, "Prophet and Pastor," *Light,* July, 1981, p. 2. This is a bimonthly publication of the Christian Life Commission of the S.B.C.
16. Wirt, p. 36.
17. Timothy L. Smith, *Revivalism and Social Reform* (New York: Abingdon Press, 1957), p. 60.
18. Charles G. Finney, *Lectures on Revivals of Religion,* William G. McLoughlin, ed. (Cambridge, Mass.: The Belknap Press of Harvard University Press, 1960), p. 287.
19. Cited by Nancy A. Hardesty, "No Rights But Human Rights," *Perkins Journal,* vol. XXXV, no. 1, Fall, 1981, p. 61.
20. Charles G. Finney, *Reflections on Revival,* Donald Dayton, comp. (Minneapolis: Bethany Fellowship, Inc., 1979), p. 113.
21. Smith, pp. 60-61.
22. See Donald W. Dayton, "Engaging the World: The Evangelism of Charles Finney," *Sojourners,* vol. 13, no. 3, March, 1984, p. 19.
23. Harry F. Ward, *Social Evangelism* (New York: Missionary Education Movement of the United States and Canada, 1915), p. 6.
24. Timothy L. Smith, "A Higher Law: Finney's Social Vision," *Sojourners,* vol. 13, no. 3., March 1984, p. 19.
25. James L. Franklin, "Church Battled Nazis with Faith," *The State,* Columbia, S. C., April 22, 1984, pp. 1A and 12A.

26. See, "A Confessional Courage: The Life of Martin Niemoeller," *Sojourners,* vol. 10, no. 8, August 1981, p. 11.

27. Ewart E. Turner, "Memories of Martin Nieomoeller," *The Christian Century,* vol. 101, no. 14, April 25, 1984, p. 446.

4
Theological Sources

Scripture Lesson: Psalm 146:1-10; 2 Corinthians 5:6-21

I agree with the Mennonite leader, Myron Augusburger who told a 1985 meeting of six Anabaptist denominations: "If you think you can be New Testament in peace and social concerns without being evangelistic, then you are mistaken."[1] On the other hand, the flip side of that would also be true: If you think you can be New Testament in your evangelism without being concerned with peace and social concerns, then you are mistaken.

Walter Rauschenbusch knew what he was talking about when he said, "The adjustment of the Christian message to the regeneration of the social order is plainly one of the most difficult tasks ever laid on the intellect of religious leaders."[2] I do not claim to be equal to the task. Nor do I propose to offer anything like a systematic theology on the subject. What I do offer in this chapter is a sketch of three theological motifs in which evangelism and social involvement may be connected.

Creation

The Bible begins with God creating the heavens and the earth (Gen. 1:1). It ends with the vision of a new heaven and a new earth (see Rev. 1—2). It begins in the garden of Eden and ends in the New Jerusalem. That closing vision has the one who sat upon the throne saying, "Behold I make all things new" (Rev. 21:5).

Believe it or not, this is God's world. He made it—matter, human beings, and all. Then, when He looked back over everything that he had made, "behold, it was very good" (Gen. 1:31). When the psalmist said he had chosen to be near God "that I may tell of all thy works" (Ps. 73:28), among those works were God's creation of the cosmos.

Psalm 136 singles out the great wonders of God's creation as an evidence of His covenant of love. We are admonished to give thanks to "the Lord," "the God of gods," "the Lord of lords," and "the God of heaven," "who by understanding made the heavens . . . spread out the earth upon the waters . . . made the great lights . . . the sun to rule over the day . . . the moon and stars to rule over the night." The psalmist went on to speak about the Exodus, the conquest of Canaan, and God's providential care over "all flesh" as evidences of His steadfast love. Twenty-six times in that one psalm is repeated the refrain: "for his steadfast love endures for ever."

Shall we despise that which God has made and which His Word tells us is an evidence of His love? If you are thinking I have forgotten about sin and the fall of Genesis 3, you are wrong. I shall come to that in due time.

Was it not this fallen creation of which the psalmist wrote in Psalm 19:1-4:

> The heavens are telling the glory of God;
> and the firmament proclaims his handiwork.
> Day to day pours forth speech
> and night to night declares knowledge.
> There is no speech, nor are there words;
> their voice is not heard;
> yet their voice goes out through all the earth,
> and their words to the end of the world.

If matter is evil, how could the good God have created it, and how can it bear witness to the glory and handiwork of God? But the psalmist was not finished. Look:

> In them he has set a tent for the sun,
> which comes forth like a bridegroom leaving his chamber,
> and like a strong man runs his course with joy.
> Its rising is from the end of the heavens,
> and its circuit to the end of them;
> and there is nothing hid from its heat (vv. 4-6).

Those are hardly the words of a sun worshiper! Nor do they come from one who has little or no regard for the Word of God. Immediately thereafter, the psalmist made some of the most beautiful references to the Word of God ever penned (vv. 7-11). Indeed, the two major points of Psalm 19 are: God is revealed in His works (vv. 1-6); and God is revealed in His Word (vv. 7-11). There is, according to the psalmist, the light without and the light within. Well might we call this the nature and law psalm.

Now, having said all of those good things about the heavens and the earth, let us not overlook the crowning act of God's creation. Again I take you to the Hebrew psalter. In Psalm 8, the psalmist looked at the heavens, the work of God's fingers. He gazed at the moon and the stars which God has established. Then, he asked: "What is man that thou art mindful of him,/and the son of man that thou dost care for him?" (v. 4). The answer to his question is:

> Yet thou hast made him little less than God,
>   and dost crown him with glory and honor.
> Thou hast given him dominion over the works of thy hands;
>   thou hast put all things under his feet,
> all sheep and oxen,
>   and also the beast of the field,
> the birds of the air, and the fish of the sea,
>   whatever passes along the paths of the sea (vv. 5-8).

Those words enlarge upon what was said in Genesis 1 about humankind made in the image of God and their having been given dominion over the creation (see vv. 26-27). They are also another form of that same cultural mandate.

You may be about ready to say to me: Well, if the first creation was all that great, why do we need a new one? A terrible thing happened in that beautiful garden of Eden (see Gen. 3). Our original parents sinned and had a great fall. They were like Humpty-Dumpty who sat on the wall. They tried to hide from God, but God Himself came and found them. He came Himself and confronted them with what they had done. God put them out of the garden, and they never found their way back.

That's not the whole story of redemption—not by a long shot. There is more, much more, and it's still unfolding right before our eyes this very moment. But perhaps enough of the story has been told for us to make a few points about how the doctrine of creation links with evangelism and social involvement.

The fall of our original parents, Adam and Eve, was so great a fall that nature itself was affected. God told Adam, "Cursed is the ground because of you . . . thorns and thistles it shall bring forth to you" (Gen. 3:17-18). Human sin was so great that it put the ground out of kilter. Apparently, nature itself fell as a result of the human fall.

Therefore, when we come to the New Testament, we read in Romans:

> For the creation waits with eager longing for the revealing of the sons of God; for the creation was subjected to futility, not of its own will but by the will of him who subjected it in hope; because the creation itself will be set free from its bondage to decay and obtain the glorious liberty of the children of God. We know that the whole creation has been groaning in travail together until now (Rom. 8:19-22).

Paul looked for a cosmic redemption in which the creation would be set free from its bondage to sin and evil. This was not some gnostic desire to escape corrupting matter because Paul was the one who said of Christ: "In him all things were created, in heaven and on earth, visible and invisible . . . all things were created through him and for him" (Col. 1:16). Almost in that same breath, the apostle to the Gentiles said, "in him all things hold together" (v. 17).

Jesus Christ is the divine glue, as it were, who causes the physical universe to cohere and hold together. Gnostics don't talk like that, only Christians who believe Jesus Christ is the divine, preexistent Logos, without whom not anything was made that was made (see John 1:1-3).

Do you suppose that voice which spoke from the throne saying, "Behold, I make all things new" (Rev. 21:5), was referring to anything like Paul's "creation . . . set free" (Rom. 8:21)? I think so because the inspired seer said, "I saw a new heaven and a new earth" (Rev. 21:1). We can be sure that our God is in the business of making *all* things new. He is making the new creature in Christ of whom Paul spoke

(2 Cor. 5:17), new persons with new hearts, new spirits, and a new song—the song of the Lamb (Rev. 5:9-10). He is making a new people (1 Pet. 2:9-10), the church, the "one new man" of whom Paul spoke (Eph. 2:15 *ff.*). And let us never forget it, God is making a new creation.

Harry R. Boer has insisted that the Holy Spirit of Pentecost and the Holy Spirit of creation belong together.

> The evangelical can forget only to his or her hurt that the Bible and with it all redemption has creation as its point of departure, as its constant focus, and the new creation as its all-controlling purpose. To confine religious and theological vision to the redemption of people with only tangential reference to the also-to-be redeemed creation is a grievous impoverishment of the gospel.[3]

If evangelists and Christian social ministers can't find common ground in creation, it may be because they have an inadequate doctrine of creation or an incomplete doctrine of the new creation. We serve Him who said, "Behold, I make all things new." His plan for the fullness of time is to unite all things in Christ "things in heaven and things on earth" (Eph. 1:10). If we want to be involved as co-workers with God in accomplishing His purpose, we shall work to make new creatures, a new community, and a new cosmos.

Sin

We are hopelessly fallen creatures. The image of God in which we were created has been so damaged that we can't repair it. All of us are flawed. The root error of Communism and all utopianism is an overly optimistic view of human nature. Our problem is not skin but sin.

We have it on the highest authority that religion can make persons worse instead of better. Jesus Himself pronounced a woe on the scribes and Pharisees for traversing sea and land to make a single proselyte but making him twice as much a child of hell as themselves (Matt. 23:15). Saint Theresa of Avila wrote about self-proclaimed saints that "when I got to know them, they frightened me more than all the sinners I've ever met." Sometimes the name

Christian goes on before the quality goes in. Yes, even Christians sin.

According to Rebecca West, James Joyce believed that in order to breathe you had to break out all the windows. Ernest Hemingway's code was that what's moral is what makes you feel good after, and what is immoral is what you feel bad after. D. H. Lawrence said his great religion was "to answer one's wants." Lieutenant William Calley annihilated My Lai to save it.[4]

Where is moral responsibility in our society? What has happened to civic righteousness and God consciousness among us? "The sin of all of us is in each of us," wrote Walter Rauschenbusch, "and every one of us has scattered seeds of evil, the final multiplied harvest of which no man knows."[5]

Sin is both individual and social, personal and corporate. All of us know what individual and personal sin is, but what is social and corporate sin? John Perkins said, "I struggle with ... corporate sins. Things like racism and oppression, injustice and inequality that create cycles of poverty and dependence for people from which there are few escapes." But he sets over against corporate sins, "the church—a corporate expression of Christ, a corporate model of his love—to break these corporate and institutional cycles and patterns that are so difficult for us to deal with alone."[6]

Corporate sin is at once both social and systemic. Take that cycle of poverty referred to by Perkins. It goes like this: "No education, poor jobs. Poor jobs, poor pay. Poor pay, bad housing and food. Bad housing and food, poor health. Poor health, poor performance on the job, less pay."[7] While poverty itself may not be sinful, it is often caused by corporate sin, and the cycle is sinful. See how sin has organized itself into structures and institutions of inequality and oppression.

None of that of course releases individuals from their personal responsibility. Both the victims and the victimizers are responsible before God for what they leave undone or have done. Nor is it a clever scheme intended to get more government welfare money. Perkins and an increasing number of others oppose government welfare programs because they victimize the very people they are designed to help.[8]

A striking example of corporate sin and evil was the My Lai massacre of March 16, 1968. Psychiatrist M. Scott Peck, who investigated the incident for the U. S. Army, called it "group evil." At My Lai, Vietnam, as many as two hundred soldiers in C Company of Task Force Barker witnessed the murder of at least somewhere between five and six hundred civilians, including women and children. Peck speculated that within one week perhaps five hundred men in Task Force Barker knew that war crimes had been committed. Yet, astonishingly, the crimes did not come to light until March of 1969. Finally, charges were considered against twenty-five men, of whom six were brought to trial. Only one, Lieutenant William C. Calley, Jr., was convicted.

Peck thinks group evil, so highly visible at My Lai, may now be the norm rather than the exception. He says we are living in "the Age of the Institution." As these institutions become larger and larger, they become faceless, soulless. "What happens when there is no soul?" asks Peck. "Is there just a vacuum? Or is there Satan where once, long ago, a soul resided?" While Peck admits he doesn't know the answers to those questions, his conclusion is that "the task before us is nothing less than to metaphorically exorcise our institutions."[9]

Perhaps the time is right to focus on those aspects of the Bible that are most alien and unwelcome to modern culture: angels, gods, demons, Satan, and the elementary forces of the universe. These have a surprising relevance and usefulness in today's world.

An open letter from Evangelicals attending the Sixth Assembly of the World Council of Churches in Vancouver in 1983 said, "Increasingly, the church is being reinforced in its perception of demonic dimensions of structural evil. They are as offensive to God and as destructive to people as any personal evil."[10]

I shall not attempt here to identify "the principalities, . . . and powers" of such passages as Ephesians 6:12. However, suffice it to say that evil is sometimes personified. Examples are Pharaoh, Ahab, Jezebel, Nero, Hitler, Stalin. "The rulers, authorities and powers of this dark world were humans not evil spirits," wrote Vishal Mangalwadi of India. "It was not the evil spirits that crucified Jesus, stoned Stephen, killed James or persecuted Paul. It was the rulers of that dark age against whom the Church was pitched."[11]

None of this dialogue about sin and evil being both personal and corporate, individual and structural is merely academic. It is of utmost importance to us and our world. "If sin can exist at every level of government, and in every human institution, then also the call to biblical justice in every corner of society must be sounded by those who claim a God of Justice as their Lord."[12]

Personal and corporate guilt are but one consequence of sin. Pastor Martin Niemoller, who spent eight years in prison for his opposition to Hitler and the Nazis, issued this famous statement:

> When the Nazis came to get the Communists, I was silent. When they came to get the Socialists, I was silent. When they came to get the Catholics, I was silent. When they came to get the Jews, I was silent. And when they came to get me, there was no one left to speak.[13]

Walter Rauschenbusch was one of those who spoke out against corporate and social sin. We should remember that Rauschenbusch began his ministry in Hell's Kitchen of New York City. He saw what the structures of society did to individuals, how those very structures ground them into the dust of the earth. His social gospel arose in the laboratory of human need. Likely the social gospel, which he so devoutly espoused, was taken too far. But he never abandoned individual salvation from personal sin. He believed the social gospel was the old message of salvation enlarged and intensified:

> The individualistic gospel has taught us to see the sinfulness of every human heart and has inspired us with faith in the willingness and power of God to save every soul that comes to him. But it has not given us adequate understanding of

the sinfulness of the social order and its share in the sins of all individuals within it. It has not evoked faith in the will and power of God to redeem the permanent institutions of human society from the inherited guilt of oppression and extortion. Both our sense of sin and our faith in salvation have fallen short of the realities under its teaching.[14]

The debate over the doctrine of sin has picked up momentum in the closing quarter of this century. Let me cite only one example, Amsterdam '83—an international gathering of several thousand evangelists put together by Billy Graham.

L. A. Yuzon, secretary for mission and evangelism for the Christian Conference of Asia, Singapore, attended Amsterdam '83 and wrote an evaluation which appeared in *One World*, a monthly magazine of the World Council of Churches. Yuzon said, "For Graham, winning souls to Christ is primary and service is secondary." He found throughout the conference a preference for the term "social *responsibility*" over "social *action*."

Yuzon's most stinging criticism of Amsterdam '83 had to do with its doctrine of sin and individualism:

> The apparently prevailing view at the conference was that, since the root of human evil is the sinfulness of men and women, the best way to change society is to change people: hence the urgency of an evangelism that aims to convert people to Christ. Little was heard of the view that changing people by the power of God's word is inseparable from the task of changing the conditions which exert a formative influence on them.
>
> A Christian cannot ignore the latter except by holding that human souls (of those saved and those to be saved) exist in a sort of vacuum, isolated from the larger community in which people live. But that is untenable in the light of the biblical insight which sees an individual as a person in community.[15]

Agapē

"By this we know love, that he laid down his life for us; and we ought to lay down our lives for the brethren" (1 John

3:16). We Christians get our definition of love from the cross, not from culture. John 3:16 should be matched up with 1 John 3:16.

An early ad for the Salvation Army read: "However poor you may be, you have two friends! One is Jesus Christ, and the other is the Salvation Army!" The whole world can truthfully sing, "What a Friend We Have in Jesus." God loved the world so much that He sent His only begotten and beloved Son to die on the cross that whoever believes in Him should not perish but have eternal life.

Agapē is a circle. It never ends, is ever enlarging, and is all inclusive. I heard in 1982 about a female prisoner in Raleigh, North Carolina, who had not had a single visitor in over eighteen months. That ought not to be. Forgotten persons need to be remembered—above all by us Christians.

When Saint Theresa of Avila said, "The nicest thing we can do for our heavenly Father is to be kind to one of His children,"[16] she wasn't referring only to Christians. She was talking about any human being. By children, Saint Theresa meant one's neighbor.

We get so hung up over phrases like the Fatherhood of God and the brotherhood of man that if we aren't careful we shall become more like the lawyer than the good Samaritan in the story Jesus told (Luke 10:25-37). *Agapē* love doesn't sit around arguing over who "the brethren" of 1 John 3:16 are or who "the least of these" are in Matthew 25:45 or who one's "neighbor" is in Luke 10:29.

God never intended for us Christians just to go around loving our own kind. Granted, Paul said, "Let us do good to all men, and especially to those who are the household of faith" (Gal. 6:10). Why did he throw that last part in? Because if we don't love our kin in Christ, chances are we won't love outsiders at all.

Is our circle of love big enough to include the whole family of God? Paul in his great love hymn said, "Love never ends" (1 Cor. 13:8). So, if we have stopped loving one another, maybe what we have is *eros* or *philos* rather than *agapē*.

Theological Sources

Jesus said if we only love those who love us, we're in the same boat with the tax collectors (Matt. 5:46).

Who is going to love the undeserving poor unless the church does? Not many. Christian charity reaches out to those to whom the government tends to write off and give up on. The worship of God involves caring for people—all kinds of persons. If we worship God, we have to touch other persons. One consultant to a 1982 consultation on evangelism and Christian social responsibility put it this way: "If we turn a blind eye to the suffering, the social oppression, the alienation and loneliness of people, let us not be surprised if they turn a deaf ear to our message of eternal salvation."[17]

Jesus gave us a love parable in the story of the good Samaritan (Luke 10:29-37). The hero of that story showed us what *agapē* love is like:

- Love finds needs and stops to help.
- Love rearranges the schedules of busy days.
- Love shows compassion.
- Love meets the needs of hurting persons.
- Love gets its hands dirty for others.
- Love pays bills and signs blank checks.

Two teenage girls were crossing the highway in Greenville, North Carolina, one Saturday night in 1982. Angela "Cookie" Radford, age fourteen, pushed her seventeen-year-old friend, Torie Lynn, off the highway. Torie Lynn never saw the small truck which was coming. Cookie saved the life of her friend, but she was too late to save her own life. Following Cookie's death, her brother commented about his sister: "She was the kind of girl who looked out for you."[18] *Agapē* love looks out for others. It makes us a keeper of our brothers and sisters.

Agapē is more than just talk; it's something we do. As Paul reminded us, "The kingdom of God doesn't consist in talk but in power" (1 Cor. 4:20). All the great nouns of our faith are verbs in the Bible. Truth, mercy, justice, and love are things we do.

I like the bumper sticker which read: "If you love Jesus, do justice! Any goose can honk." Jesus identified Himself with what He did. John the Baptist sent to Him and said, "Are you the Messiah?" Jesus answered in terms of what He did (Matt. 11:2-6).

Those who restrict Christian love to the inner life may be making a separation in the person of Jesus, between Him as Savior and as Lord. Christian ethics should not separate the two.

It costs us to love toughly, as did Jesus. Eventually it cost Him the cross death. The Christian's social conscience should be as wide and as long, as high and as deep as the love of God.

"The love of Christ controls us" (2 Cor. 5:14), said Paul. What happened on Calvary introduced a fundamental change into the moral structure of the universe. There love conquered fear, hate, injustice, and all the powers of darkness.

Agapē love is the sign equal to none that our tongues, prophetic powers, understanding of mysteries, knowledge, faith to remove mountains, charity, and martydom are genuine (1 Cor. 13:1-3). God's incredible love is sufficient to meet the incredible needs of humankind. But there is a crying need for us to be credible. If our theology is so "good," what is it doing to correct the "bad" things of our world?

Notes

1. Quoted in "Historic Peace Churches Seek a New Evangelistic Emphasis," *Christianity Today*, vol. 29, no. 8, May 17, 1985, p. 44.
2. Walter Rauschenbusch, *A Theology for the Social Gospel* (New York: Abingdon Press, 1945 ed.), p. 7.
3. Harry R. Boer, "The Holy Spirit and Church Growth," in Wilbert R. Shenk, ed., *Exploring Church Growth* (Grand Rapids: Wm. B. Eerdmans Publishing Co., 1983), p. 257.
4. Foy Valentine, "A Case for Responsibility," *Light*, September 1983, Christian Life Commission of the S.B.C., p. 2.
5. Rauschenbusch, p. 91.
6. John Perkins, *A Quiet Revolution* (Waco, Texas: Word Books, Publisher, 1976), p. 213.
7. Ibid., p. 88.
8. Ibid., p. 15.

Theological Sources

9. M. Scott Peck, *People of the Lie* (New York Simon and Schuster, 1983), pp. 212-253, but especially p. 251.
10. *A Monthly Letter on Evangelism,* World Council of Churches, Commission on World Mission and Evangelism, no. 9, September, 1983, p. 3.
11. Vishal Mangalwadi, "Was Paul an Evangelist or a Political Reformer?" *Transformation,* October/December 1984, vol. 1, no. 4, p. 6.
12. John Perkins, *Let Justice Roll Down* (Ventura, CA.: Regal Books, 1976), p. 195.
13. Quoted in "The Life of Martin Niemoeller," *Sojourners,* vol. 10, no. 8, August 1981, p. 11.
14. Rauschenbusch, p. 5.
15. L. A. Yuzon, "Some Unanswered Questions About the Evangelist's Task," *One World,* no. 90, October/November 1983, p. 23. A monthly magazine of the World Council of Churches. Italics are Yuzon's.
16. Quoted by Ruth Graham, "Falling Flat on One's Face," *Christianity Today,* vol. XXV, no. 20, November 20, 1981, p. 76.
17. Quoted in "Evangelicals Affirm Commitment to Evangelism/Social Responsibility," *World Evangelization,* September 1982, Information Bulletin No. 28, p. 8.
18. See, "Greenville Girl Killed Aiding Pal," *The News and Observer,* Raleigh, N. C., July 12, 1982, pp. 1C and 2C.

Section II
Contemporary Interfaces

5
Examples of Individual Christians Building Bridges

Scripture Lesson: Isaiah 9:2; Matthew 5:14-16

Some Christians are shedding light in terribly dark places. When Florence Nightingale was asked how she proposed to change the wretched situation of the nursing profession in her country, she replied, "By my example of course."

After she went to the front lines to minister to the British soldiers, she wrote back home, "If there is a hell, this is it." Cholera was rife. Almost nothing was being done for the soldiers. It was said of Nightingale that soldiers kissed her shadow as she passed by, they were so thankful for her.

I invite you to look with me in this chapter at some contemporary Christians who are like Florence Nightingale, seeking to shed the light of Christ in some of the dark places of our world. They are a few examples of living bridges between evangelism and social involvement.

The Example of Dru Graves

One afternoon as Dru Graves was leaving a migrant camp an elderly Haitian man took her hand and kissed it. In his French-accented English, he said to her, "Madame, God is pleased with what you do here."

Graves has been pleasing God by working with migrants for twenty-two years. To look at her, you might think from her regal appearance, with immaculately coiffed gray hair, that she should have been taking tea in the cool of the country club. Instead, this cultured Southern lady of Beaufort, South Carolina, is sitting at the table with a migrant family. She's eating something, she's not sure what, off a cracked and suspiciously stained plate. The room is hardly larger than a good-sized closet and hotter than a sauna. Kids, dirty and ragged, are scrambling in and out. A woman is cooking and a man sits at a small table. But this lady is relaxed and clearly enjoying herself as her laughter rings off the kitchen's unpainted walls.

Graves has learned not to worry about the food or safety. She is one of those mission volunteers who drives four thousand miles in four months without leaving her home county. The migrants come to South Carolina's Low Country around Beaufort to pick tomatoes and other crops. Mexicans, Haitians, and other hardworking poor, often a couple of hundred people, families and single persons, live in quarters that lack most conveniences. No air conditioning, no indoor toilets and showers—the facilities are quite primitive.

This majestic lady, and others like her, has expressed her compassion and love for these marginal persons by giving them health kits, clothes, food, counseling, and other assistance. Nor has the Word of God been neglected in all of this service. Graves gives out Bibles in the language of the people. "We give them that first because it's the best gift we have. We want to be remembered as people who gave the Word of God," said Graves. Hundreds have made professions of faith. Dozens have been baptized.

Graves feels called of God to do this particular ministry. Her call came after a home mission study on migrant ministries. Like other longtime residents of Beaufort, she was aware of the nearly two thousand migrants in twenty-seven camps who flooded the area during planting and harvest season, but she hadn't paid attention to them or understood their needs.

Enlightened by the study, she and thirty-three other women knelt in prayer and asked God's help. They prayed that if it were God's will, they might have an open door to begin a migrant ministry.

God gave them an open door. He even sent a pioneer migrant missionary to spend a month with them and show them what to do. A problem developed, however, because some members of her church thought the migrants would bring sickness and disease into the church or would damage

Examples of Individual Christians Building Bridges

the facilities. There were also racial slurs. But by a narrow church vote, Graves and her like-minded friends won.[1]

Graves, now nearing retirement age, has discovered that God is, indeed, pleased with what she is doing. And so are all Christians who want to see the chasm between evangelism and social involvement bridged.

The Example of Hubert Line

Hubert Line builds two-bedroom houses for $12,000 and a third bedroom for $3,000 more. He directs the building of seventy-five new homes with volunteer labor in McColl, South Carolina. The building site is a seventy-year-old former textile mill village. Stripped of the textile industry in the early 1950s, the village was stripped by a deadly tornado in March of 1984. This small tract of land has for years been home for some of the poorest persons in McColl.

Line, a lay mission volunteer, organized the community's reconstruction. He works with a seventeen-church ecumenical ministerial alliance, through which donations are channeled. Families who own lots bared by the tornado contribute their savings and whatever resources they have. The ministerial alliance picks up the tab for building materials. Line contracts the house building and brings in volunteer labor.

What brought this retired construction man to a tornado-stricken town on the same night of the great devastation? The Lord called him to the task. "I've been in construction twenty-five years," said Line. "We can't all preach, but if we'd all use the little things God gives us we'd be as good a witness as any preacher."

Relationships with the town's people have not always been congenial since their great loss. Following the storm, the first reaction of the people was fear. "They hated nearly everything," said Line. "They hated their neighbors because they didn't get hit. They hated me. They hated themselves." After the hatred came greed and jealousy. Everybody wanted their house built first and biggest. These were basically good people, but that's what the tornado did to them. It'll be a long time before rain and thunder doesn't bother them.

What has kept this Christian builder on the job in McColl? He prays a lot. No amount of money could keep him at it. What it all boils down to is his love for the people and their needs. That enables him to take their anger. Besides, Line has found anew that his own life is worth something.

Most of these folk aren't associated with a church. They're hard. Many are illiterate. Line sees it as a great opportunity to offer the people more than they now have. He expressed his evangelistic concern in this Christian social mission in these striking words:

> I haven't preached here. I haven't said a word. But they know who works up here. We haven't had any lost people volunteering to build these houses. Hell's Angels haven't showed up yet, you know what I mean?[2]

The Example of Don Stanley

Don Stanley was about twelve. He was sitting on the front row in church beside his good friend Dave Walton and the other Royal Ambassadors (a Baptist organization for boys). "The preacher was preaching hellfire and damnation," said Stanley. When he gave the invitation, Don ran to the front, certain that he didn't want to die and go to hell. Nobody told him Jesus loved him or what repentance meant. They just said, "Sign this card, sit on the front row, and you'll be baptized in two weeks."

His baptism didn't take. Don got his name on the church roll but not on the Lamb's book of life. "I went down a dry sinner and came up a wet sinner," said he. "I was under the deception that I was saved and was not."

Stanley had begun playing football and baseball when he was nine. He developed into a good athlete, so good, in fact, that the Boston Red Sox offered him a contract when he finished high school. He turned it down in order to accept a baseball scholarship at the University of South Carolina.

Stanley, who had begun drinking alcohol and smoking pot in the ninth grade, continued drinking at the Universi-

Examples of Individual Christians Building Bridges

ty of South Carolina where he studied pharmacy. He also started taking amphetamines and craving them. By the time he graduated in 1971, the Red Sox were no longer interested in him.

Baseball coach Bobby Richardson told Stanley in the locker room one day, "In my heart, I feel like you are going to have trouble with alcohol. I want to tell you about a friend I met when I was sixteen—Jesus." Stanley told the Christian coach he was OK and refused the call of God's Spirit at that time.

Don Stanley returned to Spartanburg, South Carolina, and began to work with Smith-Outz Drug Store. That first year he made more money than his father and mother had ever made together in one year. He got married and thought his main calling in life was to provide his family with material things.

In 1975 Stanley bought his own pharmacy in Boiling Springs. He grossed a million a year in his independent pharmacy, became a leader in the pharmaceutical association, and an officer in civic clubs. All the while he was going to church on Sunday mornings with his wife and children. The church had even elected him chairman of the baptismal committee.

Nevertheless, the young entrepreneur continued his abuse of drugs. He was charged with conspiracy to violate the Controlled Drug Act in 1980. Faced with a possible $235,000 fine and 150 years in prison, Stanley's life crumbled in two weeks. None of his partying friends came to his aid. Fortunately he was sentenced to only three years in a federal prison. But even there behind bars, he continued drinking and taking drugs for sixteen months. They were easy to get. His hatred for those who had testified against him intensified. He denounced his country and his heritage and swore that if he ever escaped, he'd never return to America.

Stanley was later placed in a cell with another pharmacist. His cellmate tried to commit suicide. Because of the similarity in their names, Stanley had begun to think of that good friend who had been seated beside him when he went forward to escape hellfire and damnation at the age of twelve. He began to pray constantly. "I thought God had left me and would never come. I even picked up a razor blade and started to end it all," said he.

Providentially a letter came from his friend Dave Walton at that point. Walton had gotten his own life straightened out in 1975, but Stanley wasn't ready to hear him then. Now, the time was right. Walton told him that he had been praying for him for nine years. He encouraged Stanley not to give up and pointed him to Jesus.

All the barriers Stanley had erected came tumbling down that day. He prayed: "Father, I'm an alcoholic and a drug addict, but if you can save me, I'll serve you right here in a prison cell." The old Don Stanley was killed right then and there. The new man started shouting, telling the guards he had met Jesus and witnessing to the inmates in the cell block. They released him from solitary confinement because they thought he had gone crazy.

He asked for a Bible but got none. Later he found a Gideon New Testament on top of a trash can and devoured it. Seven months afterward he was ordered to a halfway house. Christmas of 1983 he was allowed to go home. His childhood friend gave him a job cleaning and washing dishes in his restaurant.

Some of the people with whom Stanley used to party came to the restaurant and asked him how life in jail was. He told them, "Prison is bad, but let me tell you about something good that happened to me there."

By early 1984 Don Stanley and his friend Dave Walton had felt led to establish a special ministry called Faith Ministries, working with young people and needy persons. They set up a Salvation Center in Chesnee, South Carolina, where clothes, furniture, and food can be acquired by the needy at little or no cost. They also have opened a small Christian book store in Chesnee. They have plans to begin a food locker in the adjoining city of Gaffney. During 1984 they spoke to 16 Gideon pastors' conferences and in 110 churches, 3 high schools, 2 junior high schools, 2 colleges, 2 statewide youth rallies, and 4 prisons.[3]

Examples of Individual Christians Building Bridges

The Example of Jim Fuller

"I believe in miracles—I am one," remarked Jim Fuller. Every Tuesday night Fuller makes his way to San Quentin, one of California's oldest and best-known prisons. San Quentin houses 3,400 inmates and is the site of all California executions. It is home for some of the most serious offenders in the state. Yet on Tuesday evening Fuller can be found inside the walls of that fortress. He goes from cell to cell encouraging, witnessing, probing, and praying. His message to the fellows there is, "You can make it—I did! Miracles still happen—I'm one myself."

Fuller used to be an inmate of San Quentin. When I first heard his story, he was preparing himself for a preaching ministry at Golden Gate Baptist Theological Seminary in Mill Valley, California.

The thirty-four-year-old student grew up in Las Vegas and was the product of a broken home. By his own admission, his was a story of crime, delinquency, drugs, and prostitution. His mom, thinking she was doing what was best, sent him away to a military boarding school when he was nine. He was homesick, felt unwanted, rebelled against the authority, and saw all of it as rejection.

Fuller's problems began in earnest when he returned home at the age of twelve. He ran away, fought at school, started smoking, drinking, taking money from his mother's purse, and then stealing and robbing. The boy never knew what church was. He went to church in reform school, but just to kill time. The only real Christian influence in his life was about once a year when he visited his grandmother in Santa Paula. She'd take him to church and pray for him. She prayed for him for twenty-seven years, but he was never in Vacation Bible School or anything like that.

At seventeen, Fuller enlisted in the U. S. Army. Three months later he went AWOL, and for the next ten years lived on the streets and in the parks of San Francisco and Hollywood. He was one of the "flower children generation," doing the scene of free sex and cheap dope. Soon he was into heavy drugs—speed, coke, heroin, To support his habit, he dabbled in prostitution, drug sales, pornography, stealing—anything to make a buck.

During those years, he was in and out of jails and hospitals. Plagued by overdoses, arrests, hepatitis, pneumonia, and the like, "It's a miracle I'm even alive," said he. Fuller's world fell apart in 1977 when he was arrested for the sale of narcotics. At the time, he lived in Golden Gate Park with his dog. They caught him red-handed.

In the Redwood City jail before being sent to San Quentin, the young criminal took a serious look at his life for the first time. "It was like hell," said Fuller. "I had no one to turn to; I couldn't even make bail; I had vivid flashbacks of guilt."

At that point, one of those miracles that we hear about took place. The prisoner found a gospel tract under his jail bunk. Reading the tract convicted him; he fell on his knees in the presence of twenty other inmates and came up rejoicing and forgiven. "I felt like a thousand pounds of pressure just lifted off me," he said.

Fuller confesses that his Christian life hasn't always measured up since his conversion. There have been times when he has slipped back because his old habits had such a grip on him. His marriage to a Christian and a new baby in 1981, along with some other factors led him in 1982 to the conviction that God was calling him to preach.[4]

What better qualified person is there to offer the gospel of hope to San Quentin's inmates than a former inmate himself? Fuller's work is a reaching out in both evangelism and social involvement.

The Example of Bob Hoehn

Bob Hoehn has two major jobs. He is Emergency Medical Services instructor at Hannibal-LaGrange College and pastor of New Hartford Baptist Church in Missouri. Hoehn has been rated consistently as one of the top emergency medical technicians (EMT) in the state. He has been pastor at New Hartford for ten years.

Hoehn attributes his spiritual success to prayer and following the example of Jesus. Christ "dealt with the whole person, their physical as well as spiritual needs," said

Hoehn. He sees a close correlation between his two vocations as pastor and EMT. When treating an accident victim in an emergency situation, his approach is to deal with "the whole human being." He refuses to see persons as merely "broken legs and heart attacks." "I try to deal with their total needs, and sometimes those needs are spiritual," said Hoehn. "I think everyone should realize that a human being has a body and a soul, and you can't separate that."[5]

The Example of John Hendrix

John Hendrix grew up in Independence, Missouri. His father suffered a stroke which left him paralyzed. That resulted in his mother struggling to make ends meet while she cared for her bedridden husband and three small children.

"We were destitute," Hendrix recalls. "We had no insurance plan. We really were living on welfare."

About that time, a young friend invited Hendrix to Sunday School at Mount Washington Baptist Church. Soon the church's men's organization found out about the family's needs.

A former pastor of that congregation said, "Mount Washington kept that family going." The Brotherhood ministered to them in practical ways. They gave food and renovated the house. They conducted weekly worship services at the elder Hendrix's bedside.

Hendrix testified, "I don't know what would have happened to us if the church hadn't taken us under their wing." At the same time, the Hendrix family was a blessing to the Brotherhood of the congregation.

Through the caring ministry of Mount Washington, Hendrix came to know Christ as his Lord and Savior. Hendrix's needs and those of his parental family were met by the church.

Upon graduation from high school, the church offered to help Hendrix pay his college tuition. While in college, he sensed a call to vocational Christian service.

As Hendrix reflected on his story, he said: "Baptists had a way of discovering our kind of people. We became their people." He went on to observe, "Somehow I felt that I would pay back their investment."[6]

Has he paid back that investment? You be the judge. Today John Hendrix serves as the Basil Manley, Jr., professor of Christian education at The Southern Baptist Theological Seminary in Louisville, Kentucky. Prior to being called to that post, Hendrix served with distinction on the staff of the Baptist Sunday School Board in Nashville, Tennessee.

I do not marvel that Professor Hendrix teaches his students to value their personal stories. We are what we are because of the way God makes Himself known to us through His people. Let us salute John Hendrix and the Mount Washington Baptist Church for showing us how evangelism and social involvement can be put together.

The Example of Sam and Ginny Cannata

Dr. Sam Cannata is a medical missionary who uses his skills to treat Kenyan patients and to translate the New Testament into Murle (mor-leh). The fifty-five-year-old career missionary and his wife, Ginny, have shown concern for physical needs throughout a twenty-seven year career. They have persevered through political upheavals and imprisonment while continuing work in medical missions, literacy evangelism, and discipleship training.

"I've seen thousands of patients, preached thousands of sermons, and done a lot of things in my career," said the physician turned translator. "But if Ginny and I can help leave a tribe of people a New Testament—the Word of God —which they can read and understand, it'll be our biggest contribution."

The Cannatas have not ceased to care for the physical needs of persons. They had worked among the neglected Murle while serving in the Sudan. Ninety-nine percent of the Murle are illiterate. Mrs. Cannata had taught them to read and write, and Dr. Cannata had worked as a physician. Both had emphasized evangelism and discipleship training which resulted in a church. Then, furlough time came. It was difficult for the Cannatas to leave because the Murle had only partial Scripture portions available to them.

Examples of Individual Christians Building Bridges

During their furlough, the Wycliffe Bible Translators asked Southern Baptists' permission for the Cannatas to return to the Sudan to salvage a Murle translation project which had stalled for lack of personnel. Nine books of the New Testament had already been translated into Murle. The Cannatas were able to build upon that foundation. They returned to the Sudan, but were unable to return to their people or household goods at Pibor Post, which rebel activities had sealed off. After seven months they had to move from the Sudan to Kenya because of increasing rebel hostilities.

Some jokingly call their new base of operations in Kenya, "The Sudan Baptist Mission in Exile." But there Dr. Cannata practices medicine among the slum dwellers near Nairobi two days a week. The rest of the week, he translates the Bible for his beloved Murle.

Three times political problems have caused this couple to lose most of their possessions during a move. "The Lord has taught us that material things don't really mean that much," said Cannata. In 1977 the physician spent sixteen days in a Communist prison in Ethiopia before he and his family could leave the country.[7]

What is it that has taken them to Zimbabwe, Ethiopia, Kenya, the Sudan, and now back to Kenya? How do you account for this sacrificial and joyful service which the Cannatas have rendered? From where did Dr. Cannata get his gift for languages? I recall in seeking to answer such questions the words of Jesus: "Every one to whom much is given, of him will much be required" (Luke 12: 48). Then, too, Dr. Cannata himself has helped us with some answers: "I don't care what your vocation is, you should invest your life in the lives of individuals, as Jesus did, and help them grow as Christians so you can look back and see you've left something behind you."

80
Evangelism and Social Involvement

Notes

1. The facts and quotations in this example are based on William Tanner's column, "In Passing," *Missions USA,* November-December, 1984, vol. 55, no. 6, p. 75.

2. The facts and quotations in this example are based on Susan K. Taylor, " 'I Love These People,' Hubert Line Says; Proves It with Work," *SBC Today,* vol. 2, no. 11, March, 1985, p. 5.

3. The facts and quotations in this example are based on Frances Upchurch, "Childhood Friends: Don Stanley and Dave Walton Reunited for Special Ministry," *The Spartanburg Herald-Journal,* Spartanburg, S. C., December 30, 1984, p. E1.

4. The facts and quotations in this example are based on Robert J. Hastings, "A Miracle: From San Quentin to Baptist Seminary," *Word and Way,* vol. 121, no. 44, November 8, 1984, p. 3.

5. The facts and quotations in this example are based on "Missouri Pastor Accepts Role of Caring for Bodies, Souls," *Word and Way,* vol. 122, no. 4, January 24, 1985, p. 3.

6. The facts and quotations in this example are based on "Experience in Seminary Classrooms: Hendrix Values Personal History," *The Spire,* Winter, 1985, p. 5. Published by Midwestern Baptist Theological Seminary, Kansas City, Missouri.

7. The facts and quotations in this example are based on a Baptist Press release, "Doctor Turns Bible Translator to Help Tribe Read the Word," *Word and Way,* vol. 121, no. 33, August 23, 1984, p. 6.

6
Examples of Local Churches Building Bridges

Scripture Lesson: Isaiah 43:1-13; Acts 1:6-11

George Sweazey wrote a book in 1978 called *The Church as Evangelist*.[1] I believe Jesus Christ is the evangelist par excellence, but God has raised up the church as the continuing body of Christ in the world. Therefore, the church as an extension of the incarnation is to carry on what Jesus Christ did in the days of His flesh.

And what did Jesus do? He preached good news to the poor; proclaimed release to the captives; the recovering of sight to the blind; set at liberty those who were oppressed; and proclaimed the acceptable year of the Lord (see Luke 4:18-19). Jesus' church should do no less; "As the Father has sent me, even so I send you" (John 20:21), said He.

This chapter is about local churches which continue what Jesus did in the days of His flesh. G. K. Chesterton was right, "Nothing is real until it is local." A much less-educated person put it like this: "If you ain't nothing at home, you ain't going to be much out yonder."

We shall examine two churches in some depth and then look at a collage of churches. My primary interest is to lift up some models from which we may learn, not to exhibit perfect examples of churches which are living bridges over the troubled waters of evangelism and social involvement.

Bronx Baptist Church, Bronx

Bronx Baptist Church is located in South Bronx.[2] Founded as a mission of First Baptist Church (S.B.C.), Brooklyn, in 1964, in 1985 it had 382 active members. The Reverend Samuel G. Simpson, a native of Jamaica, was the founding pastor.

Simpson has been working hard for more than two decades to preach and practice a wholistic gospel in the

Bronx. He told me in 1985 that he was just then beginning to get the relationships needed with community leaders, politicians, and others to accomplish his dream for the Bronx. According to this seasoned pastor, a commitment of ten to twelve years is necessary in order to build effective relationships in his kind of context.

South Bronx is eighteen miles square, strewn with bricks, chips, and rubble, connected by streets like farm roads on which no one lives and no street lights burn. It has been the anathema of politicians, the bane of city planners, and the confounder of urban sociologists.

Perhaps 1,200 buildings have been abandoned. Acre after acre, block after block, towering buildings have been gutted by fire and smeared with graffiti. In the two years between 1977-1979 vandals, frustrated tenants, and landlords seeking insurance claims, set an estimated 7,000 fires. Simpson said, "The crippling thing is you could see . . . the fires blazing and couldn't do a thing."[3]

Squatters occupy empty buildings. They bathe in the streets and build fires in oil drums to keep warm. I saw vacant lots piled with rubble several feet deep. Simpson says, it is "probably the most devastated area in the nation's cities." Some have likened South Bronx to devastated Berlin at the end of World War II.

The physical devastation is surpassed only by the human suffering and deprivation. "Crime came in like a jackal does to a dying animal," commented George M. Sands, administrative assistant to a NYC councilman. "Mass exodus created a vacuum, and social ills were never dealt with."[4] Banks "redlined" neighborhoods. Insurance companies charged exorbitant premiums. Basic amenities of life, such as housing, employment, and education, were lost. The borough has more than one thousand homeless youth. Lutheran pastor, Ron Balint said, "It's impossible to calculate the extent of the needs here. People have multiple needs."[5]

Perhaps that kind of context will help us to understand why Simpson argues that "you cannot evangelize a man's soul and leave out his body." On the other hand, this visionary pastor argues with equal insistence that those Chris-

Examples of Local Churches Building Bridges

tians who minister to the body should also evangelize the soul.

Bronx Baptist Church (BBC) is known as an evangelistic church, and their pastor is widely acclaimed as a warm-hearted evangelistic shepherd.[6] When BBC celebrated its tenth anniversary as a fully constituted church in 1976, Vincent Thompson wrote: "I am happy to say I have found God to be real since he came into my heart ten years ago. It happened at Bronx Baptist Church. If you are looking for the peace that passeth all understanding, let Jesus come into your heart."[7] Many members in BBC could duplicate that testimony.

Apart from persistent and intentional evangelism, BBC would not have survived, let alone thrived and grown in South Bronx. Simpson told his congregation in 1976, "The purpose of the journey is to serve the Master with steadfastness and to recruit souls for the Kingdom as we journey on."[8]

BBC was actually started in prayer meetings in the apartment of Cecilia Robinson. They soon found a small two-family house at 2024 Honeywell Avenue in the West Farms district. Christian men voluntarily labored with their own hands to put that house into shape for a place of worship. Seven Christians committed themselves to the vision on November 6, 1964.

> From the very first week we conducted Sunday School, morning and evening services and midweek prayer meeting. Within the year three auxiliaries were formed: Training Union, Brotherhood and Woman's Missionary Society (Baptist Women). Visitation and witnessing were a dominant feature of our outreach. Invited friends, when they saw the depressed community and the shabby little building, were taken aback. But they entered, fell in love with the Word proclaimed and the warmth of the fellowship, and stayed on to become workers.[9]

Exactly two years later, the group had grown to sixty-four members. On that day, November 6, 1966, they moved from mission status and constituted into a church. They outgrew the Honeywell location and relocated in April of 1970 to their present facilities on 187th Street in the heart of South Bronx. With the help of the Home Mission Board of the Southern Baptist Convention, the congregation purchased the building formerly used by Bethlehem Covenant Church. Presently BBC is raising funds for a major expansion program which calls for the purchase and development of additional property across the adjacent street.

That brief history of BBC opens up for us several aspects of their approach to evangelism. They use the Sunday School to evangelize, but not as much as more traditional Southern Baptist churches in the South. BBC's Sunday School reaches more children and youth than it does adults. In this environment, many tend to identify Sunday School more with children and youth. The adults respond better to the term "Bible study" and to Bible study groups.

A public invitation to confess faith in Christ is offered in all worship services at BBC. Although the worship center has a divided chancel, that came with the building, in 1972 the church was able to install a baptismal pool. Pastor Simpson called the baptistry "a landmark" for his people because they had done without one of their own for eight years.

Sunday worship at BBC is a bit formal in comparison to many Southern Baptist churches. The choir is exquisitely robed; the female singers wear hats (as do some female worshipers in the congregation); they and the pastor enter the sanctuary from the rear in a processional, joyfully singing. But the dignity of the worship does not dampen the spirit of the service. Nor does it quench the passion of the preacher. Freedom characterizes pastor and people; and the service may last for awhile. They don't watch the clock as carefully as some worshipers.

BBC has all of the church programs and youth group organizations usually found in a church its size. They are unapologetically Southern Baptist and proud of their denominational identity. Each of these organizations or groups is a possible point of entry into the kingdom of God and the church. They use youth groups, choirs, and everything else they have to get persons saved and active in the church.

I have found, however, that BBC departs from the traditional Southern Baptist approach to evangelism in a number of ways. One of these has to do with prayer. Since 1970, the church has had a "Midnight Prayer Meeting." This is a group which meets every Thursday from 8:00 PM to midnight. Just read this one testimony:

> Six years ago I gave my heart to the Lord at Bronx Baptist Church. My growth as a Christian comes from the midnight prayer meeting. It has done wonderfully for me, helping to bring my wife to know Jesus. The prayer group to me is the cornerstone of the fellowship.[10]

Another departure is in the use of Continuing Witness Training (CWT).[11] Presently B. J. Ranscheart, a Mission Service Corps worker assigned to BBC, is using a modified version of CWT with parents of the church's Day Care and Learning Center.

Planting new churches may be the most effective kind of evangelism practiced by BBC. The congregation has sponsored three missions: Honeywell Avenue Chapel (South Bronx), 1970; Wake-Eden Chapel (Northeast Bronx), 1972; and Community Gospel Chapel (Parkchester), 1976. Wake-Eden had 182 active members in 1985 and is an indigenous, thriving congregation. Simpson was the founding pastor for Wake-Eden and continues in that role. Honeywell continues as a mission at Bronx Baptist Church's first location, but has its own pastor. BBC was also instrumental in sponsoring into affiliation with Southern Baptists an interdenominational fellowship at Co-op City in 1974.[12]

Simpson's vision is to start a Bible study, led by trained lay people, in each of the sixteen community districts of the Bronx. He also wants to start Bible studies among such target groups as the West Indian cult called Rastafarians, Spanish-speaking people, and Jewish people. He hopes some of these studies will develop into mission chapels and eventually into indigenous churches.

BBC's evangelism is orientated to the laity. The gifts and

talents of many members are used in the church services and activities. This includes men, women, youth, and children. Renewal evangelism with its emphasis on new life, a Christian life-style, spiritual gifts, and relational evangelism, has captured a significant number of BBC members. Pastor Simpson sees himself as an equipper of others for their work of ministry (see Eph. 4:12). His leadership style is self-consciously patterned after Jesus Christ the loving Suffering Servant. Simpson believes that the church is Christ in you where you are.

When I visited BBC in 1985, a number of the members had just finished participating in a lay renewal weekend with Saint John Lutheran Church nearby. They were so excited because they had been discussing the possibility of linking with Saint John in a ministry to street people. The Saturday night before I arrived, the young people of BBC had conducted a service in which more than twenty decisions were registered, seven of them for baptism.

Pastor Simpson uses terms such as "demonstration evangelism," "issues evangelism," and "sweat evangelism" to describe the evangelism which he advocates. By *demonstration evangelism* he means living out the gospel, being and doing the good news to which our lips bear witness, becoming a sample of what we preach, teach, and sing.

Issues evangelism is a term coined by Simpson. He thinks we can address evangelism around certain issues like housing, crime, sanitation, health care, and energy. So, there is a Medical Fellowship in BBC. This special group of hospital workers is recognized, organized, and commissioned to "make their services available to the needy and project the need and ways and means for medical workers to relate to the whole man." BBC is located near a hospital.

Simpson saw new housing development as an evangelism effort. His idea was to put one of his members on each floor of the housing development. They were to belong to the housing association and participate in it. Also, a couple of his members were placed in the office force. Along with other items all new residents were given a copy of the *Good News Bible* with an invitation to call Bronx Baptist Church if they needed help. That was a mistake because BBC did not have the staff to handle the calls.

Periodically BBC will plan and host special community meetings. One such meeting was held on September 26, 1981, at 3:00 PM. Attractive brochures were printed and sent, inviting the community to participate. The program consisted of a panel of fourteen community representatives from the borough president's office, the 46th precinct, community planning board no. 5, chamber of commerce, Fordham road development, health care, city planning office, sanitation department, Con Edison, local grocery store, community churches, and Shepherds' Restoration Corporation.

Simpson would call that kind of grass-roots community meeting "issues evangelism." It helps establish credibility for the church, gives it larger visibility in the community, provides a needy service to persons, and may enable the church to build meaningful relationships with some of the participants. If you are looking for a point of contact with your community, issues evangelism may be something to consider.

What, then, is *sweat evangelism?* It is helping paint a church building when your main work is being an architect. It is taking advantage of your opportunities to witness while you do that work. Christians pay their way to wherever a church needs help. Whatever skills they have are freely offered to the needy individual, group, church, or organization. In some cases, such as work with the Shepherds' Restoration Corporation in South Bronx, sweat evangelism can be converted into what is called "sweat equity." A dollar value is actually assigned to the labor and credited to the Shepherds, thereby enabling them to borrow more money and buy more property to help people.[13]

One sterling example of sweat evangelism is Ray Boggs from Okeechobee, Florida. Boggs has done carpentry, roofing, window and door repair, weather stripping, and just about everything else with BBC. "He doesn't just talk about Jesus," said Simpson, "he does it while he's pushing a paintbrush or swinging a hammer."

Boggs was helping remodel a church in the Bronx when a young woman who had been an alcoholic since age nine came by. He stopped his work and listened to her problems. They read Scripture and prayed for nearly two hours. Right there, in the middle of paint cans and drop cloths, he led her to know Jesus Christ.[14]

BBC is so deeply involved in both evangelism and social concerns that it is difficult to tell where one ends and the other begins. Terms like *demonstration evangelism, issues evangelism,* and *sweat evangelism* have brought that truth into focus.

Their biggest social involvement nowadays may be in the Bronx Shepherds' Restoration Corporation. Back in 1977, after all the talk about rebuilding the Bronx, a group of pastors noticed that the church had been left out of those plans. Deciding to consolidate their efforts, and knowing that no one church had the power or resources to turn the tide, the pastors got eighty-seven churches together and formed the Shepherds' Restoration Corporation. They chose housing, employment, economic development, and evangelism as their primary goals. They became involved in rebuilding their city with the people who called it home.[15]

Sam Simpson and his people have been involved with Shepherds from its genesis. Today Simpson is president of the organization. The group has been partially funded by the state of New York and New York City and has received private grants from the Council of Churches of New York City and laypersons of the Southern Baptist Convention. They have provided jobs for over one hundred fifty persons and been instrumental in helping a number of high school delinquents go back to school, while developing on-the-job training skills.

According to Simpson:

> The Bronx Shepherds currently manage six buildings. These buildings receive federal funds for restoration of all mechanical systems. The Shepherds have monitored restoration performed by contractors, have organized and set up tenant associations, and have acted as managing agents for

the buildings. The Shepherds main concern, as a nonprofit organization, is to help stabilize these buildings and offer consultation to tenants who mainly have low-income backgrounds. By stabilizing the buildings, the block and community surrounding them are improved and stabilized. These buildings are eventually given back to the tenants as low-income cooperatives.[16]

Critique

BBC links evangelism and social involvement so well that wherever you see them engaged in either they will likely be involved simultaneously in the other. Artificial distinctions are not made by them between the two, although they enthusiastically affirm the validity of each.

The church is involved almost daily in day care, food distribution, nursing home ministry, prison ministry, and housing needs. On the other hand they witness as they go and wherever they go. Bronx Baptist Church and Wake-Eden Baptist Church together baptized fifty-two persons in 1984. Their goal was one hundred. Through their actions, they have shown their commitment to an evangelism which multiplies churches as well as individual disciples.

BBC is good at networking. They know how to link with others to accomplish their mission. Their involvement in Shepherds' Restoration is a shining example of their ability to work with other Christians and government officials to rebuild South Bronx. They have been a welcome channel through which many Christian volunteers have invested themselves and their resources in the Bronx.

Sam Simpson is himself a human bridge between evangelism and social involvement. Jokingly called the "Baptist Bishop of the Bronx," he does have a network of relationships which enable him and his people to superintend some of the rebuilding of South Bronx. Simpson is also active in the Council of Churches of the City of New York. He has served as a president of the Council of Churches. He and his wife, Lola, are a formidable team, working together to drive away the darkness and bear witness to the light of Christ in the Bronx.

BBC has insufficient staff, facilities, and equipment to grow much beyond their present size. Parking space is next to nonexistent. But in spite of all that, the church continues to seek and save and serve the lost.

How can they press on in the midst of the hostile environment of South Bronx—with all of its sensory deprivation? An answer may be found in the large and colorful mural of the ascension of Christ painted on a wall of their worship center. Jesus is ascending into heaven. The eleven faithful apostles are kneeling, looking up at Him, and reaching out with their hands toward Him. That scene in Acts 1 (see vv. 6-11) is almost brought to life before our eyes. We can nearly hear our Lord saying: "It is not for you to know times or seasons which the Father has fixed by his own authority. But you shall receive power when the Holy Spirit has come upon you; and you shall be my witnesses in Jerusalem and in all Judea and Samaria and to the ends of the earth" (Acts 1:7-8).

Hominy Baptist Church

Hominy Baptist Church is anything but a typical Southern Baptist Convention grits-and-eggs congregation in Western North Carolina. Founded in 1812, the church truthfully calls itself "The First Baptist Church in Candler, N. C.," although its mailing address is actually Route 3, Box 257, Candler, N. C. 28715.

One big difference between Hominy and most surrounding churches is its ten community ministries. These are:
(1) Hominy Day Care Center
    Daily, 7:15 AM-5:30 PM
    (Child care for ages two to four)
    Scaled fee for services
(2) Hominy Pre-kindergarten
    Daily, 9:00 AM-Noon
    Classes for three-and four-year-olds
    Tuition charged
(3) Hominy After-School Care
    Daily, 3:00-6:00 PM

Examples of Local Churches Building Bridges

       Care for schoolage children for working parents
       Fee charged
(4) Hominy Summer Day Camp
    Daily, 7:30 AM-6:00 PM
    Care for schoolage children for working parents
    Fee charged
(5) Nutrition/Fellowship Program
    Daily, 9:30 AM-2:00 PM
    Age sixty and up
    Activities and noon meal
    No charge (contributions accepted)
(6) Meals-on-Wheels
    Daily, Monday-Friday, Noon
    Volunteers deliver hot meals from church to shut-ins, elderly, etc. where needed. No charge (contributions accepted)
(7) Girl Scouts (three troops)
    Weekly, as scheduled
(8) ABCCM (Community Christian Ministry)
    Volunteers at 201 Broadway
    Fourth Monday, 8:00 AM-Noon
    Budgeted Financial Support
    Collection of food and clothing
(9) Food Stamp Distribution Center
    Monthly, first Tuesday
    9:30 AM-4:00 PM
(10) Mother's Day Out
    Wednesdays, 9:00 AM-2:00 PM
    Small fee charged

The word *daily* in all of these refers to Monday-Friday. Please note in item (2) that the church does not compete with public school kindergarten. Item (3) is geared to public school children kindergarten through grade six. Item (6) currently provides fifteen meals per day. Most of those are to nonchurch members. Item (8) is a broad-based ecumenical community Christian ministry in nearby Asheville, North Carolina. The church donates annually 2 percent of its budget to this ministry plus food, clothing, and volunteers. The ABCCM stands for Asheville Buncombe Community Christian Ministry.

Item (1) up to 1985 was more a matter of providing building space and equipment to a local government-funded organization. However, because of government cutback in funds, the church has now taken over that ministry and integrated it into a systemic umbrella organization with other community ministries. The church will secure its own license to legally operate the day care center. Item (9) is a ministry of providing an office where governmental representatives can interview persons.

You will note that five of the ministries are geared to children and parents, one to senior citizens, and the other three to needy individuals of all ages. If they seem heavy on child care, that may be because North Carolina has more working mothers than any other state in the union, 65 percent. The national average is 55 percent. That makes a ministry like day care very practical.

A second thing which sets off Hominy from the typical grits-and-eggs congregation in the South is its focus on faith primarily for living instead of faith primarily for dying. Hominy does not use the highly deductive approaches to evangelization, such as the Roman Road, E.E. (Evangelism Explosion), or C.W.T. (Continuing Witness Training). Pastor Werhan sees such methodologies as focusing more on the hereafter than on the here-and-now.

Dr. C. Fred Werhan, the church's pastor since January 1, 1973, feels very strongly that the church should express its faith by loving and caring for its neighbors. He makes no difference between the evangelistic mandate and the cultural mandate. Werhan would even merge together into one the twin love commandments of Matthew 22:37-40. He sees John and Paul boiling them down to one in essence in 1 John 4:20-21 and in Galatians 5:14 (see also Rom. 13:8), respectively.

Nevertheless, the church does issue a public invitation to Christian discipleship following each Sunday's worship service. Occasional revival meetings are held, but they focus more on renewal than on outreach and evangelism. The

Examples of Local Churches Building Bridges

main structured approach to evangelism is through the Sunday School outreach program. There is an outreach director and outreach leaders in the Sunday School classes and departments. Also, a prospect file is maintained. Even so, most of the church's prospects are those who first visit their church. The church does not visit from door-to-door to discover prospects.

Furthermore, opportunities are given to children in Vacation Bible School and in the Summer Day Camp to confess their faith in Christ. Very little follow-up, however, is done on prospects discovered through these two activities. By and large the church is doing a good job evangelizing its own children and youth. Most of its additions though are through biological and transfer growth.

A third point of difference I found at Hominy was an unusual openness and sensitivity to the dignity, worth, and value of persons. This church takes the priesthood of every believer with great seriousness. A printed church brochure says it is a community of Christian faith:

> Where every person is considered free before God to find a personal faith within a community of supportive love where individual differences are respected.
> Where the Lordship of Jesus takes priority over doctrinal and creedal adherence.
> Where the Word is made flesh through a caring ministry to the full needs—spiritual, mental, social—of those about us and around the world.

According to that same brochure, Hominy is there for two reasons: "To help you find a meaningful faith . . . To provide you a place of service to God and your fellowman."

Over the past twelve years (1973-1984), Hominy has added 372 new members, 118 of those by baptism and 45 by statement of faith from other denominations, who in many Baptist churches would have been required to be rebaptized by immersion for membership, a practice which is not required by Hominy. Total membership has grown from 646 to 708 during that period. Sunday School attendance averaged 236 in 1973 and 222 in 1984. Fifty percent, or 185, of the new members are now active resident members of the church; 41 percent have moved away from the area; and 9 percent have become inactive resident members.

Critique

Hominy is strong on Christian social ministries but a bit weak on evangelism. Both the pastor and the people are fully aware of this. Presently, they are doing some long-range planning in which they hope to find and build an indigenous model of evangelism to balance their social ministries.

They do unapologetically emphasize the word *Christian* in all their ministries rather than the word *social*. A full-time, experienced church staff member has now been employed to coordinate all of the various child-care ministries under one umbrella. This position, along with other child-care staff, is supported fully from tuition and fees. The church provides the facility rent free. Some families are assisted by the local DSS on day-care fees.

There is little or no Christian social action being done corporately by the church. Their involvement is more with individuals and as individual Christians in service functions. The congregation is not involved corporately with such things as the peace movement or with public protests against racism, apartheid, abortion or United States involvement in such countries as Nicarauga.

Hominy has little intentionality about bridging social ministries with evangelism. So far, not much has been done to find and follow up on prospects for discipleship through the social programs. I believe the church has a desire to minister wholistically to persons, but may be neglecting some of the spiritual needs of individuals and their families. My judgment is that they could use more intentionality in both evangelism and social involvement.

The pastor and his leadership are a great asset to the social involvement of Hominy. Dr. C. Fred Werhan grew up in nearby West Asheville Baptist Church and left a staff position in his home church to become pastor of Hominy. He was educated at Carson-Newman College and Vanderbilt

Divinity School. The fact that he knows the area so well, has been pastor of Hominy for a dozen years, and has both a heart and head for incarnating love for one's neighbor, has greatly enhanced the church's social witness to the community. He has led the church to be a host rather than a guest to the community.

Hominy may need more willingness to take the initiative in the evangelization of their community. The church seems to now need greater balance, symmetry, and proportion between social ministries and evangelism; more intentionality in its evangelism; and a more wholesome and intelligent evangelism than it now practices.

Such balance seems to be forthcoming with the church's adoption of "New Directions," the result of a recent long-range planning effort. These included renewed emphasis over the next three years on spiritual development, evangelism, and world missions, while continuing a strong Christian social ministry.

The definitions in the church-adopted statement reveal a move toward more symmetry and proportion between social ministry and evangelism.[17] Those definitions also reveal an effort to blend the two more effectively into a wholistic approach where evangelism and social ministry are not viewed as two separate ministries for the church, but necessarily tied together as one expression of the whole gospel. Pastor Werhan believes that the "active love" manifested through the Christian social ministries of the church is both the primary expression of the means used of God to call people to salvation and the primary expression of the result of God's salvation in people's lives. "God, through love, expressed in Jesus Christ," said Werhan, "calls mankind to a salvation which is experienced through following Jesus Christ in love for others."

A Collage of Local Church Examples

"People who accept the authority of the Bible," wrote Sherwood Eliot Wirt in 1968, "are beginning to outgrow a limited approach to the basic social problems of twentieth-century living." Wirt, who was then editor of *Decision* magazine, went on to say: "The typical Gospel church of our day is not the fundamentalist enclave it was at the turn of the century."[18] The variety of examples which follow will show that Wirt knew what he was talking about.

God's Rainbows

Pine Grove Baptist Church in Rockingham, North Carolina, has a Sunday School class called God's Rainbows. The class had sixteen enrolled in 1985, ranging from age six to twenty-five. Five years ago the class began as a Vacation Bible School group for exceptional children. From June to January of that first year no one attended the class. However, the pastor and four women who started it had a vision of reaching mentally handicapped children and their parents for Christ and His church. They continued to pray, invite, and prepare. Then, they enrolled their first pupil. Next, four from one family were enrolled.

What have been the results? One of the sixteen has been saved and baptized. One was awaiting baptism when I visited the congregation in 1985. Four parents have been saved and baptized. One was awaiting baptism. God's Rainbows attend the church worship services following their class session each Sunday morning. Once each year they plan and lead the worship service for the congregation. Each summer the church takes them to a Happiness Retreat at Camp Caraway for three or four days. All of their expenses are paid for by the church.

Pastor Wayne Tuttle told me that on the average the children have to attend two years before their parents will begin to attend. A church van picks up the class members each Lord's Day. The one thing they seem to need is special literature.

The class has afforded the congregation an opportunity to minister concretely and wholistically to the participants and their families. One seven-year-old class member needed braces but lacked $900.00 having the necessary funds. Pastor Tuttle took up an offering of $1,200.00 one Sunday for that one child.

Probably for each mentally handicapped child or youth,

you will find two or more additional family members who don't attend church anywhere, according to Pastor Tuttle. This is a ministry which requires great patience and investment for long-term gains. Many loving congregations can link evangelism and Christian social involvement with a class such as God's Rainbows.[19]

Samaritan's Inn

An innovative ministry called "Samaritan's Inn" was started in 1980 by a group of six Lutheran churches. They now rent several apartments at Wakefield Apartments near Wake Medical Center in Raleigh, North Carolina. Persons with sick relatives in city hospitals or institutions can stay at Samaritan's Inn for $5.00 per night, or less if they are destitute. Three apartments were being provided in 1981, with plans for a fourth. They are for persons who couldn't afford to rent a motel for an extended period of time. The idea began when the Reverend John Costello learned of a couple who lived in their car in the Wake Medical Center parking lot all winter so they could visit their daughter in the hospital. A total of 220 persons from as far away as California had used the Samaritan's Inn by early fall of 1981.

Church members often stock the refrigerators and pantries with food. They donated some of the furniture. One church member checks on the needs of persons using the inn each day.[20]

This is certainly more presence evangelism than it is verbal proclamation of the gospel. Nevertheless, it is that incarnational witnessing which authenticates our words. Moreover, this kind of ministry obeys the injunction of 1 John 3:18, "Little children, let us not not love in word or speech but in deed and in truth."

Seeking the Welfare of the City

Third Baptist Church in Saint Louis, Missouri, is located in the heart of downtown Saint Louis. Third Baptist thrived during the Second World War. In 1948, it had over 6,000 members. By 1984 membership had dropped to about 1,900. Why the drastic decrease?

Between 1950 and 1980 the population of Saint Louis city was cut in half, from 800,000 to 400,000. There was a massive exodus to the suburbs following World War II. The suburbs swelled and the downtown dwindled. The G. I. Bill made it possible for returning soldiers to purchase homes and cars in the suburbs.

Third Baptist didn't decline so much as the neighborhood declined. Persons were able to worship in the suburbs. Some were afraid to come downtown because of the blacks, the crime, and the boarded-up buildings.

In 1984 Third Baptist celebrated its one hundredth year of ministry at its location on Grand and Washington. The church refused to move to another location like many other congregations. Today, it is part of a total redevelopment scheme for the midtown area. As the neighborhood is being renovated, the church building is being renovated, and the congregation renewed. Members have voted to raise $1.2 million for several projects. A portion of the funds, $20,000, will be used to refurbish the triangle park that stretches between Third Church and the Fox Theatre. That amount, in effect, will be a gift to the city by the church.

Pastor Ian Chapman has described Third Baptist as "multiracial, multicultural, multiethnic." The membership is far from being "a cookie-cutter congregation." Its members range from persons on welfare to millionaires, from street persons to corporate executives, and people from around the world. The church has demonstrated its commitment to the community especially through its Service Center which provides food, showers, and clothing for about fifty homeless men every day.[21]

Third Baptist had a staff member with evangelism in his portfolio long before the local church vocation of minister of evangelism became popular. The congregation's commitment to the gospel and to the welfare of the city reminds us of the words of Jeremiah: "But seek the welfare of the city where I have sent you into exile, and pray to the Lord on its behalf, for in its welfare you will find your welfare" (Jer. 29:7).

Legal Aid Clinic

LaSalle Street Church on Chicago's Near North Side has operated the Cabrini-Green Legal Aid Clinic for over a decade. Mostly financed by LaSalle Street Church, the clinic grew out of the study and experience of Charles Hogren, an attorney and member of that congregation. Hogren had studied with his pastor, William Leslie, the biblical concept of justice. They found more than eighty passages conveying God's concern for social justice.

The clinic has a staff of four lawyers and two law students. It now handles 250 to 300 cases annually. Cabrini-Green is a public housing project of 13,000 residents, more than eighty buildings and 3,600 apartments crammed into a five-by-eight block area. Average family size is five persons; and 70 percent of the families have only one parent, who is often a woman younger than twenty-five who had her first child by age fourteen. About the only role models come from the three "Ps" of prostitution, pimps, and pushers.

Social structures have not been changed by the Legal Aid Clinic. But a Christian presence and ministry has been established. The church is present with the poor in their struggles. Some youth have been changed. But much more remains to be done.[22]

Night Care for Children

Mulberry Baptist Church in Charlotte, North Carolina, began "Mulberry Night Care" in 1983. Members and prospective members can purchase a "Freedom Pass" which entitles them to eight hours of child care at the church any time from 6:00-10:00 PM on Monday, Tuesday, or Thursday of each week. This service enables parents to have supervised child care for their children birth through third grade while they go shopping or spend some special time together.[23]

This congregation is noted for its strong commitment to evangelism. It has experienced rapid growth during the last decade. Something so elementary as quality night child care for a few hours might put a church in contact with a network of potential disciples. Churches who extend loving care to children will gain the attention and interest of their parents.

Notes

1. George E. Sweazey, *The Church as Evangelist* (San Francisco: Harper & Row, Publishers, 1978).
2. Bronx Baptist Church is located at 331 East 187th Street, Bronx, New York 10458. Phone number is (212)933-4095.
3. Quoted by Celeste Loucks, "The Shepherds of the Bronx," *Home Missions*, vol. 50, no. 1, January, 1979, pp. 4-11.
4. Ibid., p. 6.
5. Quoted by Judith Klein Erdmann, "The Gospel Is Alive and Well and Living in the South Bronx," *The Christian Century*, vol. 101, no. 39, December 12, 1984, p. 1174.
6. I shall use BBC as an abbreviation for Bronx Baptist Church.
7. *Tenth Anniversary Souvenir Journal*, 1966-1976, Bronx Baptist Church, p. 27.
8. Ibid., p. 3.
9. Ibid., p. 5.
10. Ibid., p. 27.
11. Continuing Witness Training (CWT) is the name of a lay witness training program used by Southern Baptists. It seeks to equip Christians to share their faith personally and face to face. For more information on CWT, write the Home Mission Board of the SBC, 1350 Spring Street, N. W., Atlanta, GA 30367, or call (404)873-4041.
12. See *Tenth Anniversary Souvenir Journal*, p. 5.
13. Samuel G. Simpson, "Bronx Shepherds' Restoration Corporation," *Church Administration*, vol. 26, no. 6, March 1984, pp. 25-27. An amount of over $85,000 was assigned to the labor of SBC volunteers up to March of 1984.
14. Quoted and related by Mary Knox, "Redneck Encounter," *World Mission Journal*, Vol. 52, No. 8, August, 1981, p. 4.
15. See, "The Church at Work," *Metropolitan Church News*, vol. 55, no. 6, December, 1984, p. 4. This is a publication of the Council of Churches of the City of New York.
16. Simpson, pp. 26-27.
17. Hominy's "New Directions" definitions are as follows:
   Spiritual Development is a process of growth toward Christlikeness . . .
   Initiated by a personal faith in, and commitment to, Jesus Christ as Savior and Lord;
   Continuously renewed through disciplined efforts to allow the Spirit of God as revealed to control more and more one's life;
   Resulting in a changed inward experience of life, characterized by the fruits

Examples of Local Churches Building Bridges

of the Spirit (love, joy, peace, patience, kindness, goodness, faithfulness, gentleness and self-control (see Gal. 5:22f), and a changed outward expression of life, characterized by actions of love for others and the world.

Evangelism is being, doing and telling, among those with whom we have personal contact, the good news of God's salvation for their lives and their world, available through faith in, and commitment to, Jesus Christ as Savior and Lord . . .

Expressed through intentionally seeking to help others find, experience and live the abundant, eternal "life in Christ," characterized by an inward experience of the fruits of the Spirit and an outward expression of love for others.

Accomplished by God's Spirit bearing witness through us, as we seek to live as Jesus lived, to love as Jesus loved, and to proclaim Jesus Christ as God's Way, Truth, and Life for them.

World Missions is being, doing and telling, with others beyond the limits of our normal personal contact, the good news of God's salvation for their lives and their world, available through faith in, and commitment to, Jesus Christ as Savior and Lord . . .

Expressed through seeking to help all the peoples of the World find, experience and live the abundant, eternal "life in Christ," characterized by an inward experience of the fruits of the Spirit and an outward expression of love for others.

Accomplished by the witness of God's Spirit through missionaries who live among them as Jesus lived, who love them as Jesus loved, and who proclaim Jesus Christ as God's Way, Truth, and Life for them;

Made possible through our prayer-wrought support, which leads us to give sacrificially and go ourselves at God's calling.

18. Sherwood Eliot Wirt, *The Social Conscience of the Evangelical* (New York: Harper & Row, Publishers, 1968), pp. 2-3.

19. On April 14, 1985, Pine Grove Baptist Church had 466 enrolled in Sunday School and 227 in attendance. The church is located at 907 Airport Road, Rockingham, North Carolina 28379.

20. See John Robinson, "Kin of Wayfaring Patients Find Samaritan's Inn Home," *The News and Observer,* Raleigh, N. C., September 20, 1981, p. 34I.

21. Gigi Schrader, "Commitment to St. Louis Prompts Church Facelift," *Word and Way,* vol. 121, no. 13, March 29, 1984, p. 4.

22. See Rodney Clapp, "Housing Project Lawyer: Taking Christ's Social Concern Seriously," *Christianity Today,* vol. XXVI, no. 11, June 18, 1982, pp. 60-61 and 64.

23. *The Mulberry Message,* vol. XII, no. 11, March 16, 1983, pp. 2-3. Published by Mulberry Baptist Church, 6450 Tuckaseegee Road, Charlotte, NC 28214.

7
Examples of Parachurch Organizations Building Bridges

Scripture Lesson: Amos 5:24; Romans 8:1-4

Consider with me now three parachurch organizations which have reputations for trying to link evangelism and social involvement. The three I have chosen are Christian Rehabilitation Center in Charlotte, North Carolina; Emmanuel Gospel Center in Boston, Massachusetts; and Voice of Calvary Ministries in Jackson, Mississippi. I shall seek to describe and critique each model respectively. Then, I shall do a brief combined summary on the three.

Christian Rehabilitation Center, Charlotte

"Three hots and a cot," that's the way clients used to describe the typical gospel rescue mission. From its founding in 1936, until perhaps eight years ago, that phrase might have been a proper description of Rebound. But Rebound is today far more than three hots and a cot.

Its official name is now Christian Rehabilitation Center, but it is better known by its short nickname of Rebound. Located at 907 West First Street in Charlotte, North Carolina, Rebound has had four locations.[1] In 1966 Rebound moved to its present location, a two-block facility formerly owned by Standard Oil Company. Today that property is worth perhaps $1.5 million and appreciating rapidly, partly because $90,000 condominiums are going up across the street.

This old Charlotte Rescue Mission was founded by conservative and fundamentalist Christian laymen. The fathers of evangelists Billy Graham and Grady Wilson were active in the work of the mission. Melvin Graham, Billy's brother, is now a board member. Those earlier locations were closer to uptown and were more like storefronts. One was actually a former brothel.

Examples of Parachurch Organizations Building Bridges

So much of the "plus" in Rebound's change of direction and image is due to its executive director, The Reverend H. Gordon Weekley. Weekley came to Charlotte in 1955 as the founding pastor of Providence Baptist Church, located in a wealthy section of the city. The church grew and prospered, but somewhere along the line the pastor got hooked on prescription drugs. He became an addict to those drugs, lost his pulpit, house, cars, family, career, and almost everything else, including his self-respect. Nothing seemed to help. He ended up at that rescue mission on First Street of which he had said, "I wouldn't want to be caught dead there." Totally undone and at the end of his road in 1973, Weekley cried out to God for help. He had hit rock bottom; but through God's grace and the assistance of Rebound, he began to slowly rebuild his life.

Weekley became the assistant chaplain after five months. Then, about eight months later, he became chaplain to the community of alcoholics and other addicts. Eight years ago he became the executive director. Rebound, under his leadership, began to move deeper into rehabilitation and to offer more wholistic care to the clients.

Slowly, a professional trained staff has been assembled. According to Weekley, the staff has changed the direction of Rebound. Several of the staff are themselves recovered alcoholics or drug addicts and products of Rebound's caring ministry. The professional staff members feel a lifetime calling to this kind of ministry.

Rebound sees itself as a twentieth-century Christian inn, being a good Samaritan to those men who have been robbed, beaten, and left for dead along the Jericho roads of Charlotte. It has 122 beds, but, as in the first century, this inn is more than a place to sleep. It is a refuge and home for those needing help. In the past eighteen years this clean, comfortable inn has provided:

- 1.5 million meals
- 368,899 pieces of clothing
- 2,000 families helped with counseling, food, clothing, furniture
- 8,500 worship services

- 1,579 Bible classes
- 3,196 radio programs
- 1,900 jail visits
- 157,271 one-on-one counseling sessions

All of this has been done without any governmental money of any kind. Nor does the mission receive large amounts of foundation or grant money. Too many strings, Weekley feels, are attached to government and grant money.

No single denomination or church funds Rebound. The 1985 budget was $675,000. About $50,000 of that was raised by the sale of donated junk in Rebound's store. Over forty local churches contribute to the ministry. More than 45,000 individual names are on Rebound's computer mailing list. An annual banquet is held at the city civic center for Rebound's friends.

A basic premise of Rebound is that sobriety flows from a personal spiritual awakening. "Victory flows from a personal relationship with Jesus Christ," is the way Weekley put it. The heart of Rebound's program is found in Romans 8:1, "There is therefore now no condemnation for those who are in Christ Jesus." Rebound makes a spiritual response to alcoholism and drugs along with all the other responses.

Almost all of Rebound's clients are either alcoholics or drug addicts or both. They don't have to be Christians to get in or stay in. The only requirement for entrance is that they be sober and able to function in a group setting. "People hungry and hurting don't have ears," said Weekley. "What they have are needs to be met." Immediately upon entrance, the center seeks to meet the client's legal, mental, and medical problems. After those needs are met, he comes to an interview with the spiritual director.

About 60 percent of the center's clients are white and 40 percent black. Their median age is thirty-five. Some years ago most of them had alcohol related diseases. An increasing number now have mental and emotional problems. Nowadays men in their twenties are showing up, many of them hooked on drugs or a combination of drugs and alcohol. The majority of the clients are from North Carolina, most of them from a radius of 75 to 100 miles.

Residents are restricted to the center the first two weeks. Then they become eligible for weekend passes. If they come back drinking, they are not admitted but are referred to the detoxification center on Seventh Street. Each case is dealt with individually, but responsibility for one's actions is impressed upon the clients. The men are taught to be responsible for themselves and their conduct.

Clients are requested to commit themselves to stay at the center a minimum of ninety days. The staff has discovered through much experience that it takes that long to get clients ready for entrance back into the work world. Up until that time, many of them are almost like children until they are put to the test. So at the end of ninety days each is given a complete physical and put in touch with a counselor from the North Carolina Rehabilitation Department. About 12 to 15 percent of the clients go into a rehabilitation program at the end of the ninety days.

Worship services are conducted at Rebound twice each Sunday at 7:15 AM and 3:00 PM and on Tuesday and Thursday evenings at 7:00 PM. Those hours are chosen so as not to interfere with the men's participation in local churches.

The chapel will seat several hundred persons. It is clean, attractive, well-lighted, and air conditioned. The podium is on the same level with the congregation, but removed a few feet beyond the first row of seats. Folding theater seats arranged in rows fill the room, rather than pews. A King James Version of the Bible has been provided by the Gideons for each seat rack. A large cross backdropped by a soft light adorns the front of the auditorium. That cross is the only Christian symbol in the room, except for the Bibles and hymnbooks. Above the speaker's podium is a huge, three-word sign which reads CLAIM YOUR MIRACLE.

Critique

Rebound is seeking to incarnate the amazing grace of God about which John Newton wrote in his hymn. Gordon Weekley and his staff bear continuing witness that God is greater than all the powers of darkness. Sin, death, the grave, and hell are no match for the God of glory who has unveiled Himself in the face of Jesus Christ. These faithful witnesses are saying in a hundred or more ways to many persons, "God loves you and we love you too." If I were to pick a theme song for Rebound, it would be "What a Friend We Have in Jesus."

The Queen city has one thousand or more broken men wandering her streets. In Charlotte, only Rebound and the Salvation Army minister wholistically to these hurting men. Mecklenburg County is embarrassingly short on ministries like Rebound.

The dignity of human beings is affirmed at Rebound. They never call street persons bums, drunks, drug addicts, acid heads, hoboes, or the like. Persons are called by their names. Most of them have been talked down to and mistreated for such a long time that they have lost their own sense of value and dignity. Their feelings have been tranquilized. The staff at Rebound listens to them with empathetic ears.

Christianity is not forced on the residents of Rebound. The men are not "preached to" or pressured to make a premature decision to follow Christ. Each one is personally counseled about his spiritual condition. Each is required to attend the fifteen-minute devotions at 7:15 every morning and to attend the worship services on Sunday and on Tuesday and Thursday evenings. Also, during the first week in the center, all clients spend their afternoons in a discipleship program. After that requirement is met they choose between work therapy groups and the five-week-long discipleship curriculum. Approximately 35 percent of the men choose to go through the rigorous discipleship program.

Another strength of Rebound is its sixteen-member board of Christian laypeople. These men and women constitute virtually a who's who among Charlotte's business, professional, and church leaders. One board member is Linwood Stroud who is a graduate of Rebound.[2] Each brings to the rotating board (three years on and one off) his or her expertise in such areas as administration, finances, fund raising, public relations, nutrition, and health care.

Rebound is truly an arm of the local churches in Charlotte. It works alongside them and extends their caring hands. It is better located geographically to minister to these men than most of the city's churches. It has the facilities, the theology, and the staff to complement the churches' mission to male alcoholics and drug addicts. Many volunteer opportunities for social ministry and evangelism are also offered to Christians through the channel of Rebound.

We might also speak a good word about Rebound's intentional networking with other helping agencies in Charlotte. The staff knows what services are available through others and doesn't hesitate to use those services. They work hard trying to meet all of the varied needs of their clients. If they can't meet those needs themselves, they usually know who can.

Rebound is certainly not a perfect model. The present staff makes no claim to perfection. Let me mention several areas where they may need to improve. They need more black staff members, especially since 40 percent of their clients are blacks.

They may need to exhibit more concern for a comparable ministry in Charlotte to women. Once Rebound sought to serve female clients, but it didn't work out well. Their past failure with women and their present success with men uniquely positions them to advocate a comparable ministry to women in Charlotte.

Rebound should more self-consciously see and promote itself as a model for other such centers. The time has come for Rebound to produce more substantive literature to serve the whole church.

I also believe the staff and board may profit from an in-depth consideration of whether they can do more to help the city and the churches to prevent alcoholism and drug addiction. As it is now, Rebound is tackling the problem on the back end more than on the front end. Another way of saying it would be to observe that they are now doing more Christian social ministry than social action. Perhaps that should continue to be their role. But the evils of alcoholism and drug addiction can never be fully overcome apart from a systemic approach.

I hope that each of these suggestions will help Rebound to become that wonderful place called "The Land of Beginning Again." Their heart's desire is to be faithful undershepherds of "the good shepherd" who came to bring the abundant life, and to defeat the "thief who comes only to steal and kill and destroy" (John 10:10-11).

Emmanuel Gospel Center, Boston

Finding 2 San Juan Street in Boston's South End is not easy, but that's the headquarters for Emmanuel Gospel Center (EGC).[3] Located within a twenty- to thirty-minute walk of the Boston Common, San Juan Street was called W. Canton at one time. Now, a cab driver told me, part of W. Canton has been renamed San Juan in honor of the Puerto Ricans who live there.

Boston's South End (not South Boston) was originally designed as a walking community. That area has had people living in it who spoke forty or more languages. Today Spanish is the dominant foreign language. About 60 percent of the housing is low income in the immediate neighborhood around the center, according to Dr. Douglas Hall, executive director of Emmanuel.

EGC began in 1938. That was the year of the great hurricane, colloquially called the "hurricane of '38." The vision for it as a permanent preaching station grew out of a ministry known as the "Church on Wheels," where some persons drove around with a truck conducting services. At the center, evening worship services were held, with different churches assisting.

When Hall came in 1964, the facilities were a storefront building on W. Dedham Street. The area was known as the skid row of Boston. It was a very deteriorated slum area. The Halls' salary was $2,400. Poor people helped support Doug and Judy Hall.

Today EGC is an inner-city parachurch organization which serves local churches in Boston and other urban

Examples of Parachurch Organizations Building Bridges

areas by offering various resources and also carrying out direct ministries of evangelism and meeting human needs. The Gospel Center building serves as a facility for three inner-city churches.

Cooperative ministries of Emmanuel provide services and facilitate training for lay people and pastors. Their purpose is to strengthen the local church and, through cooperation with churches, to build up the body of Christ. Cooperative ministries include audiovisual services, Christian education and conferences, the Christian leadership project, church planting assistance, Emmanuel Book and Record Shop, Fellowship Bookstore, library-research, neighborhood building use, neighborhood evangelism, resource networking, and urban ministries classes with Gordon-Conwell Theological Seminary.

Pioneer ministries of the center are those where staff members serve primarily unchurched people in a community, often in areas where there is no church active in that particular ministry. Pioneer ministries include community advocacy, youth outreach, Bible clubs ministry, Roxbury street ministry, North Dorchester nursing, and the many helping relationships of individual staff.

A legal aid clinic began operating in 1985. Haitian outreach services are now in the planning stages.[4]

One may see that ministry moves on two major tracks at Emmanuel: cooperative ministries and pioneer ministries. Cooperative ministries relate to other Christians and pioneer ministries deal directly with non-Christians and secular structures.

An illustration of cooperative ministries is resource networking. Through networking one parachurch organization can do what five or six others might be doing without networking. Nowadays networking is a big thing, especially in the cities. Simply put, networking is the process of getting the needs of persons together with the available resources.

Two of EGC's most effective networks are "Urban Ministries Network" and "Love in Action." The Urban Ministries Network is a communications system which aids in meeting the informational needs of urban churches and ministries across the country. It is a way of exchanging information on useful resources, tested strategies, and principles of urban ministry. The network informs members of effective models of ministry and educational opportunities through its Network Newsletter. Inquiries are answered with EGC's own informational resources and by networking persons through referral to other urban ministries. Emmanuel's own resources include an excellent urban church library, research tools and guides, and occasional papers and resource reviews.[5]

Love in Action is the social component which grew out of the Billy Graham Boston crusade in 1982. Charlie Glenn was asked to develop this social arm of the crusade but would not consent unless EGC was involved. Emmanuel did get involved when Hall became convinced that an instrument could be created which would last beyond the crusade. In cooperation with other Christian leaders, Love in Action has continued. Its primary purpose is to network suburban and urban churches and Christian groups in a cooperative effort to meet the needs of both poor persons and the churches and organizations that minister with and to them. This purpose is achieved in three ways:

- By producing and distributing a catalog of mission opportunities in eastern Massachusetts.[6]
- By mobilizing Christians to carry out more effective mission in the name and power of Christ.
- By developing a vision for the calling of God to "seek justice" and "correct oppression" (Isa. 1:17).

An illustration of pioneer ministries is the Roxbury Street Ministry. This is an ongoing ministry carried out by Ronald "Pete" Lumpkins and his wife, Charlotte. They are committed to crisis counseling in relation to drug and alcohol abuse, juvenile delinquency, domestic problems, and released prisoners. Their ministry is strongly evangelistic and practical. It includes sharing their home with people in crisis situations. The Lumpkins have seven children.

Emmanuel evangelizes directly through open-air evangelism and church planting. For sixteen years the center has done open-air evangelism with the aid of a specialized mo-

Examples of Parachurch Organizations Building Bridges

bile stage unit on a trailer pulled by a van. This open-air witnessing is always done cooperatively with churches in the areas where the trailer is set up.

Church planting is done with planters from the denominations. EGC, for example, has worked with Conservative Baptists to plant a network of congregations. Several churches have actually used the center's facilities until they got strong enough to move into their own facilities. On any given Sunday you may encounter three congregations worshiping in the center throughout the day.

According to Hall, Boston has a low percentage of churches. If you are trying to plant a church in a deteriorated area, unless you have a strong ethnic group, it can take a long time. Hall thinks it can take six years before such a mission can become a church. If relationships have broken down because of crime, poverty, and so forth, a lot of community development may be necessary before a church can be established. The glue for a new church has to be more than the church planter. However, the planter initially is the glue of this kind of church community; and, if he leaves too soon, the work can suffer. Therefore, church planting tends to be a wholistic ministry.

Emmanuel's board of directors is denominationally diverse. It includes such groups as Presbyterians, Episcopalians, and Assemblies of God—about seven different denominations altogether. The interdenominational center operates only in Boston.

EGC has close ties with Gordon-Conwell Theological Seminary. Hall took the initiative to establish ties with his alma mater. The seminary has two programs in Boston. One is an urban extension program for urban pastors and Christian workers which uses the center's facilities.[7] The other Gordon-Conwell program is a one-year experience in the city of Boston for students in an urban training program. Hall teaches the core courses on urban ministry in this program.

Hall and his staff all live in the inner city. Each person has to raise his or her own financial support before joining the staff. Presently there are fourteen full-time staff members, but there are other associates and volunteers. EGC does provide a tax-deductible financial channel for all designated funds. Also, some financial assistance is provided toward staff retirement benefits, health care, and sabbaticals. All monies designated for a specific area go to that and nothing else. EGC is a "faith-mission" operation in terms of finances.

Hall graduated from Moody Bible Institute, earned a B.A. and an M.A. degree in counseling from Michigan State University. He earned his B.D. at Gordon-Conwell and also was awarded an honorary D.D. by that school. Presently he is a member of a Conservative Baptist church that meets in the Gospel Center's building.

Critique

Emmanuel is well named. The word means "God is with us." It is beyond doubt an incarnational ministry which fleshes out the gospel before the eyes of the poor. Day after day, in season and out of season, EGC's staff lives out the good news in Boston's South End.

Eighteen years ago Hall walked through a housing project with a child who yelled out his Sunday School memory verse, "I have been crucified with Christ!" (Gal. 2:20) The child was from a very difficult family situation and he had known multiple problems in his young life. Hall said:

> I never forgot that very unusual walk through the projects that day, and really did not know what was going through Gary's mind when he yelled out that verse. But, when he came up from Miami, Florida, last week to tell me about his wonderful wife and family and all that he was doing for the Lord 1,700 miles away, and that his main life's verse is Galatians 2:20, then I began to realize what God meant when he said, ". . . my word . . . shall not return to me empty" (Isa. 55:11).[8]

The Living Bible is not just the name of a paraphrase of the Bible; it is a descriptive phrase for Christians, the body of Christ, serving God in today's world.

The staff is unapologetically evangelical and evangelistic,

Examples of Parachurch Organizations Building Bridges

without being narrow-minded and uptight about their faith. They have a conservative theology but are not hung up on any one methodology. No one can accuse them of "morphological fundamentalism," or the fundamentalism of form.

Those staff members whom I met are very relational and hospitality oriented in their ministry. They spend a lot of time with persons—all kinds of individuals and groups. They know others and are known by others in the community. Even some of the little children knew Doug Hall.

I mentioned hospitality. The Lumpkins with their seven children aren't the only ones who share their home with others. When I visited in the home of Doug and Judy Hall, there was a young man living with them temporarily. Across the years the Halls have had over five hundred persons live with them!

You sense the teamwork of Doug and Judy Hall. They are a strong support to each other. Both are unconditionally committed to Jesus Christ and faithful to their vocation in the inner city.

Emmanuel ministers wholistically in deed and word, in example and telling, through being and doing, with life and lips. I believe EGC is a worthy model of Christian servanthood and life-style in Boston. This ministry exhibits a wholesome and intelligent evangelism which is in partnership with Christian social involvement.

I do, however, wonder about the wisdom of separating ministries into cooperative and pioneer ministries, especially so when in their scheme of ministries church planting is listed under cooperative ministries and yet called an evangelistic ministry. This distinction may be administratively OK, but it is not consistent with the idea of pioneer ministries being directed toward outsiders. Nor does it square well with the biblical and theological understanding of evangelism. Nevertheless, I strongly affirm their calling church planting evangelism. We are called both to multiply disciples and churches.

Voice of Calvary Ministries, Jackson

"We Christians . . . are trying to convert people without loving them," wrote John Perkins. "We're trying to say that we love people's souls but we have no concern whatsoever about their bodies." Perkins continued: "In Mississippi, whites today have often come to me saying, 'John, I love your soul.' But I answer, 'My soul is in a black body. And if you really want to get to my soul, you're first going to have to deal with this body.' "[9]

Those words from the founder of Voice of Calvary Ministries (VOC)[10] reveal how Perkins sees the relationship between evangelism and social involvement. Although Perkins moved to Pasadena, California, in 1981 and became the president emeritus and minister-at-large for VOC, his ideas and vision continue to permeate the organization.

When the pastor of a church in Jackson agreed not to accept black children in his church's day-care program, Lemuel S. Tucker, president of VOC since 1981, commented: "Loving your neighbor has become an optional part of the gospel." Indeed, Tucker uses the analogy of skim milk versus whole milk to describe his theology of evangelism and social involvement. The question then becomes, who put the fat into the milk of the gospel and who took it out. According to Tucker, evangelism without partnership with social involvement is skim-milk theology. VOC has opted for a whole-milk theology which puts evangelism and social involvement together.[11]

How does VOC put the two together? One answer may be found in this parachurch's statement of purpose:

> The purpose of Voice of Calvary Ministries is to live out the principles of relocation, reconciliation, and redistribution in the process of Christian community development, to develop several target Mississippi communities of need and to use these developed target communities as replicable models for wholistic ministry training in other cities and regions of the U. S. and the world.[12]

Note those three R's in the purpose: relocation, reconciliation, and redistribution. They are what Perkins calls the

Examples of Parachurch Organizations Building Bridges

three R's of community development, and they sum up the essentials of VOC's approach to ministry.

Relocation is almost synonomous with incarnation. "Jesus Christ RELOCATED from the riches and glory of heaven to the ghettos and sin of earth."[13] VOC believes that in order to minister effectively to the poor, Christians need to relocate in the community of need as part of a local body of believers; that Christians should see themselves as the replacement of Christ's body here on earth in the community where they live.

John Perkins and his family were following the principle of relocation when they moved from Pasadena, California, to Mendenhall, Mississippi, in 1960, from Mendenhall to Jackson in 1974, and from Jackson back to a decaying area in northwest Pasadena in 1981. "We must identify with, live among, and actively seek out those who are poor and oppressed and relocate our bodies and hearts with those who enjoy no human rights," wrote Perkins, "because that's just what Jesus Christ did."[14]

Relocation enables us to live as neighbors with the poor. The needs of that neighborhood become our own needs. Shared needs and friendships become a bridge for communicating the gospel and working together for better conditions in the community.

Reconciliation involves evangelism and discipling. The love and forgiveness of the gospel reconcile us to God. VOC believes that "all people are sinners by nature and by choice and are incapable of returning to God apart from faith in Jesus Christ."[15] There is no greater chasm than that between God and sinful humankind.

Spiritual rebirth is the beginning of right values. Perkins got saved and was reconciled to God at age twenty-seven. That's what brought him back to the state where his older brother Clyde was shot and killed in 1946 by white law officers. Then, in 1970, after ten years of engagement in the ministry of reconciliation, Perkins was jailed and nearly beaten to death by local white law officials who were determined to put an end to his efforts.[16]

Out of that experience of suffering, he learned that love

is stronger than hate. Later, he wrote: "As a Christian, my responsibility was to seek to be reconciled. Then out of that reconciliation, justice would flow." Perkins continued, "True justice could come only as people's hearts were made right with God and God's love motivated them to be reconciled to each other."[17]

The gospel also calls for reconciliation with our neighbors. The local church is called and sent to be "a force and forum" for reconciliation. "We seek to promote lasting reconciliation across racial, cultural, social, economic and other barriers that can hinder the reconciled life of the church," says one of VOC's documents, "by coming together as blacks and whites in work, worship and shared lives in the Body of Christ."[18]

Redistribution is following Christ's call to share with those in need. It means more than the redistribution of our goods. A sharing of our skills, technology, and educational resources is also needed. That sharing should be done in a way that empowers persons to break out of the cycle of poverty and become able to meet their own needs.

Perkins has made much of what he calls the "felt-need concept." Jesus, for example, met the felt need of the woman of Samaria in John 4. She felt the need for dignity and self-respect. Jesus met that need by asking a favor of her.

Perkins doesn't mean we are always going to be able to meet persons' felt needs. Nor does he want us to force ourselves into the lives of others and presume to know what their needs are. Instead:

> We should come to them in love, listen to how they perceive what their needs are, and then love them around those needs. Never should we think that we know what people's needs are and that we can force these conceptions on them.[19]

VOC considers most welfare programs "dehumanizing." How can we blame the poor for food stamps and welfare, one staff member argued. The poor did not invent such programs nor do they control them. The organization focuses

Examples of Parachurch Organizations Building Bridges

on self-help rather than relief or long-term structural change.[20]

The three R's of relocation, reconciliation, and redistribution are seen as a strategy for bringing justice to all persons. VOC sets them forth as biblical principles which the twenty-five-year-old organization seeks to live out in witness to Christ and service to poor communities. If followed, VOC believes these principles will bring about a quiet revolution.[21]

VOC has, indeed, become a model for wholistic ministries in Mendenhall, Jackson, and New Hebron, Mississippi. In 1978 the work in Mendenhall became an autonomous model of Christian development in a rural community. The ministry there is under the direction of indigenous leadership developed during the earlier years of Perkins's work in Mendenhall. The South Central Mississippi Rural Health Association and the Christian Community Health Fellowship in New Hebron are self-sufficient ministries. VOC Rural Services, Inc., of New Hebron is growing toward self-sufficiency.

Let us return to our earlier question. How does VOC put together evangelism and social involvement? Another answer can be found in the number of community development projects which function under the umbrella of Voice of Calvary Ministries.[22]

People's Development, Inc. (PDI) is a nonprofit housing cooperative which buys and renovates deteriorating neighborhood homes. At one time, the housing construction company owned sixty-five houses. In 1984 the inventory was about twelve. The houses are remodeled and rented or sold to low-income people. PDI enables low-income persons to buy their own homes. It helps reverse neighborhood deterioration and provides persons with adequate housing.

Thriftco is a developing network of thrift stores in poor areas. The stores sell low-cost clothing and household items. Cooperative members receive discounts and yearly rebates. Thriftco's aim is to provide an economic base for the development of poor communities. It serves as an educational development center, providing community seminars in money management, vocational skills, home weatherization, and cooperative economics.[23]

VOC's Family Health Center brings health care to an underserved area. In 1984 the FHC had over 6,000 patient contacts, and the staff's goal for 1985 was to have 10,000.[24] A local board now provides leadership for the health center. It offers medical services, pastoral counseling and pharmaceutical services. Health outreach programs concentrate on nutrition education and preventive health care. The cost at the health center is about one half of what would be paid at other doctors' offices.

The John M. Perkins International Study Center[25] is the educational arm of VOC, introducing, training, and maintaining people in understanding the mission of VOC, with the ultimate goal of producing community developers prepared to implement and advocate the three R's of Christian Community development. Several two and one-half day Christian Community Development Workshops are offered annually for pastors, teachers, and other interested persons.

The study center also seeks to develop the leadership abilities of young people. One-on-one and small-group discipling are utilized with student interns who come for the summer. Eight summer interns were present when I visited ISC in 1984. They were Lutherans, Methodists, Episcopalians, and American Baptists.

ISC equips present and future church leaders to become wholistic community developers by sharing the experience and vision of VOC. Students receive on-the-job training through participation in the ministries of VOC. Also, the study center conducts a volunteer program that includes opportunities for college students and other individuals to learn by working with VOC.

Other projects sponsored by VOC include the Northwest Pasadena Ministry, a Computer Learning Center, Youth Leadership Development and Child Evangelism Ministry. VOC's Youth Leadership Development ministry shared the gospel with over eight hundred children and young people between the ages of five and nineteen in 1984. VOC's intensive summer program in 1984 combined child evangelism, youth discipleship, tutoring, and recreation to reach over three hundred neighborhood youth.

Critique

Child evangelism has been, and continues to be, a big thing with VOC. John Perkins had good reasons to be kindly disposed toward Child Evangelism Fellowship. His wife, Vera Mae, was saved through CEF as a young girl and had always loved their use of flannel boards. Right after he was converted, a lady on his street invited him and his wife to attend Child Evangelism classes with her. Soon both he and Mrs. Perkins began teaching CEF classes among black children of Monrovia each afternoon at 5:00 and going to leadership training workshops every Tuesday night. At those workshops, they began to learn the Bible and met white Christians for the first time. In fact, Wayne Leitch was Perkins's white teacher.

A friendship developed between Perkins and Leitch which resulted in Leitch discipling Perkins. Two afternoons weekly for one and one-half hours during the next two years, they met together after work to learn, think, and talk man to man and Christian to Christian. Furthermore, Perkins had an experience with young black prisoners in California which convinced him that the best way to keep young men out of prison was through child evangelism.

Child evangelism was the first project Perkins undertook when he returned to his native state. At one point he and Mrs. Perkins were working with ten thousand students monthly![26]

Along the way, however, the Lord revealed to Perkins that black rural Mississippians weren't merely spiritually deprived. They also lacked sufficient food, clothes, houses, jobs, education, and medical care. Slowly this unusual black minister realized that the gospel he was proclaiming had to be wholistic. It had to meet not only persons' spiritual needs but their physical, social, and economic needs as well. That new realization led VOC into voter registration, marching and demonstrating, economic boycotts, economic cooperatives, and the development of health-care centers.

Doing God's work means ministering to the whole person in all of his or her relationships. VOC comes close to being a balanced parachurch model for wedding evangelism and social concern. "We've tended to emphasize evangelism exclusively," said Perkins in a 1985 interview, "so that while we have 50 to 60 million evangelical Christians, we're losing the battle against the hard problems in our society. The gospel has proclamation power as it is clothed in demonstrable concern for human needs."[27]

VOC holds together the individual and corporate dimensions of the gospel and society. The founder of VOC put it this way: "In order for the church to have the same impact as Christ and for us to become a body that is making a real difference in this world, we need to share the good news on both fronts—corporately and individually."[28]

VOC is uniquely related to a local church called Voice of Calvary Fellowship (VOCF). When Perkins relocated to Jackson from Mendenhall, on Sundays the small staff of VOC met for worship. Volunteer workers, students, and others began to fellowship and worship with them. Out of that group came VOCF.

The congregation is a growing body of Christians, both black and white. It is a living testimony to the reconciling power of Jesus Christ. Its ministries include worship, fellowship, and teaching, along with a neighborhood youth center and tutoring program.

It would be accurate to say that at the heart of Voice of Calvary Ministries is the Voice of Calvary Fellowship Church. Phillip K. Reed, the congregation's white pastor, is a member of the board of directors for VOC. Also, Lem Tucker is an elder for VOCF.

The strength of this relationship is the unusually close ties which it gives a parachurch group (i.e., VOC) to a viable worshiping local church (i.e., VOCF). One of its weaknesses is the confusion created in the outsider's mind between the two legally separate entities.[29]

VOC reported thirty-two staff members with salaries

ranging from $7,000 to $23,000 for 1984. Its total income in 1984 was $941,366, with $865,247 of that being public support.[30] It is a member of the Evangelical Council for Financial Accounting (ECFA).

I found the staff to be intelligent, articulate, friendly, and theologically conservative. President Lem Tucker is a graduate of Westminister Theological Seminary in Philadelphia and has an AME Zion denominational background. A football player in study hall at college read his Bible for thirty minutes each day. He told Tucker he read it because he was weak. That started Tucker to thinking. The seed were planted which changed him from "religious and unsaved" to saved and growing.

Another fact which may help us to understand the Voice of Calvary's theological orientation is to remember how it got its name. It comes from Calvary Bible Church of Burbank, California, and in particular from that congregation's radio broadcast called the "Voice of Calvary." Jack MacArthur, pastor of Calvary, led his people to sponsor John Perkins as one of their rural ministry representatives. The sponsorship continued for seven years. Calvary was the first group to support VOC. Galatians 2:20 also became an important Bible verse to Perkins.[31]

VOC is located in West Jackson. The immediate neighborhood is about 75 percent black and 25 percent white. Thirteen years ago those figures were reversed. Perkins picked a needy place to evangelize and minister. Many of the older persons—both white and black—feel trapped. Tucker and his key staff members live among those whom they serve.

Combined Summary

While each of these models is radically different in some ways (i.e., in size, purpose, history, and context), they have much in common. They are at the same time evangelistically and socially oriented. None is real estate hungry or has an "edifice complex." Building the kingdom of God, rather than their own kingdom, seems to be their passion.

The three are more relational than propositional in their evangelistic approach. Persons are more important to them than programs. Contacts with persons are made at their points of need. Awareness of spiritual needs is omnipresent, but physical, social, mental, and other needs may be met first. Passionately they affirm the dignity and worth of individual persons.

Hospitality looms large with them. They live among those they serve and lead. Geographical and social distance are minimized for the sake of identification, communication, and effectiveness. Servanthood is emphasized. Jesus is lifted up as the perfect model to follow. A simple life-style characterizes their leaders and staff. Their leaders make lifelong commitments, have long tenure, and are not climbing a mythical ladder of success. Frequently you see a husband and wife working together as a team among their key staff persons.

These organizations are theologically conservative but flexible in the ways they do ministry. They are experts in networking with others in order to accomplish their mission. None is dependent upon the government (federal, state, or local); yet neither is isolated from political bodies. They make wide use of volunteers and concentrate upon leadership training. Positions are open in their operations for persons whom they lead to Christ and for those who start at the bottom of life. Racial segregation is not tolerated.

Notes

1. Mailing address is P.O. Box 34648 Charlotte, NC 28234. Telephone is (704)-334-4635.

2. See, "Award Winner Lived Street Life," *News on the Rebound,* vol. 7, no. 1, March, 1985, p. 3. This is a publication of Rebound.

3. Emmanuel Gospel Center's mailing address is P.O. Box 18245, Boston, MA 02118. The telephone number is (617)262-4567. For additional information on Emmanuel Gospel Center, I recommend the well-written case study by Douglas Hall, "Emmanuel Gospel Center: Contextualized Urban Ministry," *Urban Mission,* vol. 1, no. 2, November 1983, pp. 31-36; and "Inner-City Missionary Nurse: Interview with Nurse Elizabeth Kidd, Boston, Massachusetts," *Urban Mission,* vol. 2, no. 4, March, 1985, pp. 12-21. Anyone who doubts that evangelism and social involvement can be dynamically linked together should read this inspiring interview. EGC is the abbreviation used by Hall to designate Emmanuel Gospel Center.

Examples of Parachurch Organizations Building Bridges

4. Most of the preceding four paragraphs are Emmanuel's description in the *Greater Boston Mission Opportunities Catalog*, 3rd ed., May 1984, p. 20. Coordinated through EGC, and published by Love in Action.

5. See Rudy Mitchell, "Evangelism in the City," *Urban Mission*, vol. 1, no. 3, January, 1984, pp. 30-35, for an exhibit of the kind of resources produced by EGC. Mitchell has been a staff member of Emmanuel since 1976. He is a graduate of Cornell University and Trinity Evangelical Divinity School, is director of the Library-Research Development, and coordinates the Urban Ministries Network.

6. Three editions of the catalog have been published, one each year since 1982. The third 1984-85 edition is seventy-five pages in length and is one of the finest tools I have seen for urban networking. This edition sells for $5.00. See also note 3 above.

7. See Rudy Mitchell and Eldin Villafane, "The Center for Urban Ministerial Education: A Case Study in Urban Theological Education by Extension," *Urban Mission*, vol. 2, no. 2, November, 1984, pp. 31-39, for more information on the ties between Emmanuel and Gordon-Conwell.

8. This quotation is from Hall's newsletter of September, 1984.

9. John Perkins, *A Call to Wholistic Ministry* (St. Louis, MO: Open Door Press, 1980), pp. 43-44.

10. Voice of Calvary Ministries is located at 1655 St. Charles Street, Jackson, Mississippi 39209. VOC is the abbreviation used by the leaders of Voice of Calvary Ministries in their printed materials.

11. The analogy was used by Tucker in a 1984 personal interview with him in Jackson.

12. Quoted from the "Statement of Purpose and Faith" in VOC's *1982 Annual Report*, p. 3.

13. Lem Tucker, "Biblical Speaking, Mission: Incorporated or Incarnated?" *A Quiet Revolution*, vol. 10, no. 2, Spring, 1984, p. 2. This is the newspaper published quarterly by VOC.

14. Perkins, pp. 25-26.

15. Quoted from the "Statement of Purpose and Faith" in VOC's *1982 Annual Report*, p. 3.

16. See John Perkins, *Let Justice Roll Down* (Ventura, Ca.: Regal Books, 1976), especially pp. 15-24 and 154-169.

17. John Perkins, *With Justice for All* (Ventura, CA: Regal Books, 1982), p. 102.

18. Quoted from the "Statement of Purpose and Faith" in VOC's *1982 Annual Report*, p. 3.

19. Perkins, *A Call*, pp. 42 & 44.

20. See Mark Olson, "A Giver's Guide," *The Other Side*, vol. 21, no. 2, Issue 161, March 1985, p. 39.

21. See John Perkins, *With Justice*, pp. 58-188; and John Perkins, *A Quiet Revolution* (Waco, Texas: Word Books, Publisher, 1976), pp. 217-220.

22. Perkins, *With Justice*, chapter 13, "Ten Years Later," pp. 122-137, brings together all of the ministries of VOC in Mendenhall, Jackson, and New Hebron and takes the reader on a driving (or walking) tour of each as it existed in 1981.

23. I am indebted to "The VOC Story," a brochure printed by VOC, for this paragraph.

24. These statistics are taken from President Lem Tucker's solicitation letter dated December 12, 1984.

25. The International Study Center is located at 1433 Grand Ave., and is headed

up by D. L. Govan and assisted by his wife, Helen. ISC's phone number is (601)353-5413.

26. See Perkins, *Let Justice,* pp. 74-75, 84, 91, 217.

27. Quoted by Paula Rinehart, "John Perkins and the Voice of Calvary," *Discipleship Journal,* vol. 5, no. 1, issue twenty-five, 1985, p. 22.

28. Perkins, *A Call,* p. 31.

29. Voice of Calvary Fellowship now worships temporarily in the Stringer Grand Lodge at 1072 Lynch Street. See chapter 11, "The Reconciled Community," in Perkins, *With Justice,* pp. 103-112, for detailed information on VOCF as it was intended to relate to VOC.

30. These figures are taken from an audited financial report furnished by VOC. I do not know how to account for the wide differences between this report and that of Olson, p. 45.

31. Perkins, *Let Justice,* pp. 96, 12, 70.

8
Six Models for Naming the Name of Jesus
Scripture Lesson: Isaiah 42:8; Acts 4:12

Aristides, a non-Christian, described the Christians to Hadrian, the Roman emperor, as follows:

> They love one another. They never fail to help widows: they save orphans from those who would hurt them. If they have something they give freely to the man who has nothing; if they see a stranger, they take him home, and are happy, as though he were a real brother. They don't consider themselves brothers in the usual sense, but brothers instead through the Spirit, in God.[1]

I wish that description by Aristides were accurate today. Don't you? If all Christians were really like that, the vocation of Christian social minister would probably have never come into existence. Moreover, if Christians rendered social ministries that willingly and in that kind of context, the question which I am addressing may never need to be raised.

When do you name the Name in Christian social involvement? I am of course referring to the name of Jesus Christ.

The Traditional Rescue Mission Approach

One answer is the traditional rescue mission approach. On Thanksgiving Day of 1980, for example, the Upper Room Jesus Compassionate Ministry at 4608 Troost in Kansas City, held its annual Thanksgiving dinner for many of the city's derelicts. Pastor John D. Birmingham joined the City Union Mission, the Salvation Army, and several area churches, in rounding up more than one hundred hungry men and inviting them to a feast on turkey, giblet gravy, dressing, green beans, and all the other trimmings.

Picking up the needy and the down-and-out on Thanksgiving Day and offering them a turkey dinner is something Mr. Birmingham and others have been doing for years. However, a meal is not the only gift offered to these men.

A religious service is held for them. They are expected to attend. "Our intent is to reach them spiritually," said Birmingham, "but sometimes you first have to reach them physically."[2]

This traditional rescue mission model to naming the name of Jesus is one approach which has been widely used for many years. You invite a hungry person to eat a meal or to sleep on a warm bed and, in turn, require him to attend a religious service where he is told that he can find in Jesus Christ the Bread of Life. You attach a condition to your charity. The condition is that he sit still while someone names the name of Jesus to him.[3]

The Risky-Deed-and-Word Approach

A second model to naming the Name is what I shall call the risky-deed-and-word approach. Let us look at a documented example.

Tom Eisenmann, minister of education at First Presbyterian Church in Boulder, Colorado, was returning home from a fishing trip. It was raining. He was running about two hours late. Eisenmann passed a hitchhiker and decided to go back and pick up the man.

The hitchhiker tossed his pack through the tailgate and stepped in. Though in his early twenties, the man looked older with his beard and being bent over in the downpour. Eisenmann said the young man was dirty, ragged, and soaked to the skin. His name was Lynn.

Lynn told Eisenmann that he had been traveling for more than a month from Oregon to Texas and east, up the coast, and then back to Chicago. "You have to be careful in big cities," said Lynn. "Hitchhikers are often beaten and robbed."

As Eisenmann neared the turnoff which would take him home, it was almost dark. He asked Lynn how late he would be on the road. Lynn replied that it didn't pay to get a ride after dark. His intention was to get off at the next overpass, climb to the top of the concrete bank and sleep on the ledge underneath the bridge.

Inwardly, the minister of education was being prompted to invite Lynn to his home for the night, but he feared for the safety of his family. Eisenmann's wife, Judie, was already worried because he was so late. Nevertheless, he invited Lynn to spend the night at his home.

Judie was observably nervous when her husband introduced Lynn and told her he had invited him to spend the night. However, she quickly recovered and the tension disappeared while they ate their evening meal together. Later Lynn took a shower, and they talked for about an hour. Then he went to the guest room across the hall from the Eisenmann's four-year-old daughter.

At breakfast they prayed together. Tom and Judie told Lynn how they had become Christians and the changes which had come into their lives as a result. They were surprised how they had gotten to know each other in such a short time. Lynn was taken back to the highway and went on his way.

A few weeks later a letter came from Lynn. He expressed his thanks and said he had been telling others about these Christians who had taken him in for the night. "They can't believe," said Lynn, "that there are still people in the world who would do something like that."[4]

Please note that while the risky-deed-and-word approach exemplified by the Eisenmanns is somewhat comparable to the traditional rescue mission approach, it is more costly. There is greater risk involved; it is more soft sell; and it establishes greater credibility. Also, it seems to fit much better the description of Christians by Aristides to Hadrian.

The Never-on-Rainy-Friday-the-Thirteenth Approach

Still a third approach to naming the name in Christian social involvement is what I shall call the never-on-rainy-Friday-the-thirteenth approach. When persons get down-and-out on those inevitable rainy Fridays the thirteenth, some think we must never name the name of Jesus at such an inopportune time.

An example of the never-on-Friday-the-thirteenth approach may be seen in the Christian social ministry of Chuck Lewis, a Lutheran minister who works with the Night Ministry in the seedy Tenderloin district of San Francisco.

The Night Ministry is a nondenominational emergency program operated by the Council of Churches. Lewis ministers to derelicts, addicts, prostitutes, runaways, and lonely people from 10:00 PM to 4:00 AM. He has walked the streets for sixteen years, helping and finding help for those who can't take care of themselves. He has never been attacked or robbed, although he deals sometimes with desperate and violent persons.

"Our basic theology is nonjudgmental," says Lewis. "I believe the entire world has already been saved," he said. "So it relieves me of a lot of frustration. I don't have to go out and play God every night. I just do the best I can."[5]

Even if you believe, as I do, that persons without Jesus Christ as their Lord and Savior are lost, something may be said for the never-on-Friday-the-thirteenth approach. Do we have any right to attach strings to our *diakonia*? Does *agape* ever love for what it may get in return? Is there not such a modern abomination of desolation as "buzzard evangelism"? Could Viggo Sogaard be right when he says that "effective evangelism takes place on the premises of the recipient, the place where he is in control"?[6]

A 1980 pastoral letter from the six pastors of Sojourners Fellowship in Washington, D. C., has a paragraph which bears on our subject:

> Relationship to the poor should be seen as a spiritual discipline rather than simply an occasion for ministry. We should not be measuring how much ministry the community is producing but rather how much compassion and passion we feel for our neighbors.[7]

The U.C.-J.C. Approach

A fourth possible approach to naming the name in Christian social involvement is what I shall call the U.C.-J.C.

approach. U.C. stands for Ultimate Concern and J.C. for Jesus Christ.

Once I heard a Christian leader say, "We ought to listen to another person until he tells us his or her U.C. (=Ultimate Concern), and *then* we should tell him or her about our J.C. (=Jesus Christ)."

Admittedly, this is a highly philosophical approach to naming the name. However, it may fit what 1 Peter 3:15 admonishes, "Always be prepared to make a defense to any one who calls you to account for the hope that is in you, yet do it with gentleness and reverence."

Are we giving insufficient attention to listening in our *diakonia* and too much attention to telling? Are our deeds of love and justice and mercy only intended to open up streets and avenues for dump-truck evangelism? Can persons really hear our words when they are hurting so deeply? Will we ever learn the ultimate concern of certain persons until we identify with their plight more incarnationally?

The Specialization Approach

Still a fifth model for naming the name is to recognize that certain members of the body of Christ should specialize in evangelism while others specialize in social involvement. To caricature this approach, we might say that some Christians are to specialize on naming the Name (i.e., the evangelists) while others are to specialize on *diakonia* (i.e., the Christian social ministers).

John R. W. Stott comes very close to this approach, although he uses the term "social action" rather than "social ministry." Stott thinks that this is a possible way out of the impasse which we now face between evangelism and social action (and ministry). He thinks it important to distinguish between polarization and specialization. We should accept the reality, says Stott, that God calls some Christians to specialize in evangelism and others to specialize in social action. Stott continues:

> The early church first recognized this when the apostles affirmed that their special calling was pastoral (the ministry

of the Word and prayer), while the seven were appointed to the social work of caring for the widows (Acts 6). Paul's doctrine of the body of Christ, with all members gifted for different ministries, confirms and universalizes this truth.[8]

Legitimate specialization can be prevented from further driving wedges between evangelism and social action, thinks Stott, if these three suggestions are followed: First, regardless of our specialist callings, every Christian is sent into the world as both a witness and a servant. Second, every local church should be involved in both evangelism and social action. Third, missionaries should themselves specialize in accordance with the New Testament pattern.[9]

One problem with that is that Stott does not differentiate between Christian social action and Christian social service (or ministry). Indeed, the example which he cites is more appropriately social service. A second problem with it is that one of the seven is the only person whom the Bible calls "the evangelist" (Acts 21:8). Moreover, the author of Acts clearly connects the seven with evangelism and church growth (see chs. 6—8 of Acts).

Nevertheless, Stott is on much firmer biblical ground when he uses Paul's doctrine of spiritual gifts and the church as the body of Christ to support his concept of specialization. I believe his three suggestions, if followed, can help us find a way beyond our present polarization. But I caution strongly against dichotomizing the telling and doing functions in naming the name of Jesus.

The Conversion of Structures Approach

A sixth and much more radical model for when to name the name calls for the conversion of structures and not just individual souls. The Maryknoll Sisters of St. Dominic (M.M.), one of the oldest and largest missionary orders of Roman Catholic American women,[10] demonstrate what is meant by converting structures to the lordship of Jesus Christ. Indeed, the Maryknoll order itself has been radically changed by the social upheavals of the past twenty years. Originally the nuns wore gray religious habits and black veils. They catered to the upper classes. Their goal was then "to bring Christ to non-Christians, often by staffing institutions to serve the better off, expecting that they in turn would help the poor."

Since Vatican II, Maryknoll has painfully reassessed its purpose in light of the council's emphasis on global peace and justice. Most of the sisters have discarded their robes and veils. They now live in shantytowns and barrios to show solidarity with the Third World poor. Gone are the protection and security of their convents and their religious habits. Now Maryknollers feel that working with the poor requires missionaries to change the social structures which condemn the poor to lifelong poverty.

Two Maryknoll mission sisters were raped and murdered in El Salvador in 1980. They died in the line of duty. Their commitment cost them their lives. These modern martyrs show us that mission is a total way of life.[11] When you believe something enough to die for it, such belief will inspire others to follow your tracks.

The example of poverty may also help us to see what is meant by naming the name through the conversion of structures. Look with me for a moment at poverty in Appalachia. Can poverty in Appalachia be eradicated simply by changing the individuals who are victims of it? Many think so. Even many church folk say to the poor of Appalachia what Job's friends said to him: "If you had been living right, all of this adversity would not have befallen you." John McBride, executive director of the Commission on Religion in Appalachia puts it this way:

> The breakdown comes because we can't seem to see the structures that underlie poverty today. All we Baptists tend to see is individual initiative, individual sin, and individual failure. Even when we talk about the church's responsibility, it is in individual terms.[12]

But see the other side of that individual. A bank in an Appalachian town is paid ten cents for every food stamp which it processes through its little machine. The banker is himself a Southern Baptist, but he never stops to think how his own bank profits from poverty. Yet, his bank will not lend money to the poor because they have inadequate collateral. Nevertheless, the poor can get loans at very high interest from a loan office in the same town. That loan company, with its extravagant interest rates and its quick repossession policy, is owned by a pillar of the church.[13]

Now just who needs to be changed? The poor individual? The banker? The loan shark? Surely all of them need to be changed in some ways. The structure itself needs some kind of change. Here is a real need. There is no simplistic answer. I call, therefore, for the conversion of the individual persons concerned and for the conversion of the oppressive structures involved. We have to name the Name to both.

Conclusion

The polarity of converting souls or structures is an illusion. It is unreal. And *if* there is a polarity, the poles should be seen in terms of a tuning fork. The poles of a tuning fork vibrate each other. Each pole of the fork acts as a complementary opposite, and only in this sense are they polar opposites.

Notes

1. Quoted by Jim Wallis in "Recovering the Evangel," *Sojourners*, vol. 10, no. 2, February 1981, p. 5.

2. See Faye A. Silas, "Pastor Gives Poor a Reason to Give Thanks," *The Kansas City Times*, Nov. 28, 1980, pp. C1 and C4.

3. Not all gospel rescue missions follow this model, and some who do are changing to a different model. See, for example, Lee Holthaus, "The Union Rescue Mission of Los Angeles," *Urban Mission*, vol. 2, no. 2, November, 1984, pp. 5-14; and *The Olive Branch*, vol. 90, no. 2, April, 1983, a publication of Chicago's oldest rescue mission: The Olive Branch, 1047 W. Madison St., Chicago, Ill. 60607. See also, Ralph Woodworth, *Light in a Dark Place* (Winona Lake, Ind.: Light and Life Press, 1978), for the fuller story of The Olive Branch.

However, enough rescue missions still follow this or a similar model for naming the Name that the approach described here is no caricature. For example, see Colman McCarthy, "Poverty Seen Firsthand: Homeless in a City with Little Shelter," *The News and Observer*, Raleigh, N. C., January 27, 1983, p. 4A, for a vivid description of the approach used by Pacific Garden Mission in Chicago. Compare that article with McCarty's sequel to it, "Shelter for the Homeless: 'Criminals of

Six Models for Naming the Name of Jesus

Poverty' Spend Night in Jail," *The News and Observer*, Raleigh, NC, February 2, 1983, p. 4A.

4. See Tom L. Eisenmann, "Loving the Unlovely," *Decision*, November 1980, vol. 21, no. 11, p. 6.

5. See Pete Jacobs, "Theology Is Nonjudgmental for Night Minister, Helpers," *Spartanburg Herald*, Spartanburg, SC, December 31, 1980, p. A8.

6. Quoted by Barry Tetley in "Unstructured Evangelism," *World Evangelization*, Information Bulletin No. 21, December 1980, p. 3.

7. See Jim Wallis, "Over the Long Haul," *Sojourners*, vol. 10, no. 1, January 1981, p. 26.

8. See John R. W. Stott, "Saving Souls and Serving Bread," *Christianity Today*, vol. XXIV, no. 19, November 7, 1980, pp. 50-51.

9. Ibid., p. 51.

10. The Maryknoll Sisters of St. Dominic (M.M.) were founded in 1912 in the state of New York. They are the unofficial counterpart of the Catholic Foreign Mission Society of America, which was founded in 1911 and is also known as Maryknoll Missionaries. See *The Official Catholic Directory ANNO DOMINI 1981* (New York: P.J. Kennedy and Sons, 1981), pp. 975 and 1049; and *New Catholic Encyclopedia* (New York: McGraw-Hill Book Co., 1967), vol. 9, pp. 396-399.

11. See "Sisters of the Third World," *Newsweek*, December 22, 1980, p. 75.

12. See "Rich Mountains, Hungry People," *Seeds*, vol. 3, no. 9, October 1980, p. 81.

13. Ibid., pp. 8 and 9.

Section III
Future Interfaces

9
Point-of-Need Evangelism
Scripture Lesson: Isaiah 58:6-9*b*; Luke 10:25-37

I should like to offer in this chapter a typology of personal evangelism which may enable us to better understand the polarization which now exists among us.[1] My hope is that this approach will enable us to eliminate some of the polarization. While my scheme of thought is directed toward personal evangelism, it has implications for social evangelism, and some points of overlap with what Virginia Ramey Mollenkott has called New Age Evangelism.[2]

A Typology of Personal Evangelism
(Intentionality)

Type I	Continuum	Type II
Point-of-Need		*Propositional*
Conversational	vs.	Confrontational
Life-style	vs.	Lip
Fresh	vs.	Canned
Spontaneous	vs.	Memorized
Relational	vs.	Rationalistic
Household	vs.	Hit
Presence	vs.	Proclamation
Target Group	vs.	Shotgun
Web	vs.	Individual
Net	vs.	Hook
Long-term	vs.	Short-term
Affirmation	vs.	Anxiety
Discipling	vs.	Decision
Kinesthetic	vs.	Noetic
Service	vs.	Soulwinning
Everyday	vs.	One day a week
Inductive	vs.	Deductive

135

Commentary on the Typology

Two major types of personal evangelism are available to us: *Point-of-Need* (Type I) and *Propositional* (Type II). These types exist on a continuum running from left to right. The types tend to gather under the two poles labeled Point-of-Need and Propositional. Seventeen contrasting words (or phrases) are listed under each type to help identify the respective poles. Each of the thirty-four words is intended as an adjective; for example, discipling evangelism contrasts with decision evangelism.

These descriptive adjectives are chosen because they are, for the most part, the actual ones used in the literature on personal evangelism. Almost every one of the lot could be footnoted and tied to one or more authors.[3]

I list point-of-need evangelism first because it came first chronologically. Moreover, I believe it best represents the methodology of Jesus and the apostolic church. Furthermore, even the staunchest advocates of the propositional approach, such as James Kennedy who created Evangelism Explosion, agree that the goal of all lay witness training is to make life-style witnesses out of Christians.

If either negative or positive feelings are kicked up as you ponder the diagram, that may help you to understand comparable feelings expressed by others regarding the two approaches. Evangelism does generate feelings, some of which are very strong.

Generally speaking, we might say that point-of-need evangelism tends to see the gospel as wrapped up in the person of the living Christ to be relationally presented and to be assented to incarnationally; propositional evangelism would tend to view the gospel as a set of true propositions to be rationally presented and to be assented to intellectually. Type I would be more informally caught than formally taught; Type II would be more formally taught than caught.

Certain persons, both disciples and prospective disciples, are more kinesthetic or feeling oriented. On the other hand, some of both would be more noetic or mind oriented. That should give us some clues as to which type of personal evangelism we should employ.

Type I is more contextually focused; Type II gives the appearance of evangelizing individuals in a vacuum. The first type points to the organic nature of society, while the scond appears to see persons only as discrete individuals.

Point-of-need evangelism is more geared to persons who are low in their receptivity to the gospel; but the opposite holds for propositional evangelism. I asked a group of about forty Christians in Edison, New Jersey, in 1985, "If we went out right now to share the gospel with undiscipled persons in your community, what percent of them would be receptive to our message?" None answered more than 5 percent. Most said not over 3 percent. Some thought less than 1 percent. Ask yourself and your friends what they think about that question. If less than 10 percent of the people are receptive to the gospel, what does that tell us about which type of personal evangelism we need to employ most frequently?

If we find ourselves in emergency situations with persons where time is critical, a short-term propositional approach might be more appropriate. However, if long-term relationships are called for, then Type I might be more appropriate. In broad terms, we can say that Type I is more concerned with what the New Testament calls *kairos* time, or seasonal time; but Type II can be characterized by *chronos* time, or chronological time. Another way of putting the same thing would be to say those who go with Type I invest more for long-term capital gains, while those who choose to use Type II invest more for short-term gains.

The propositional approach will appeal more to creedal-type Christians. I have talked with a number of persons who said their faith had become clearer and more meaningful to them through the study of a propositional approach such as Evangelism Explosion or Continuing Witness Training. So far, the lay witness training programs of Type II have been more systematized and better packaged. This type requires considerable discipline. One of its strengths is that it provides its practicioners with a definite technique to follow once a prospective disciple is brought under conviction by the Holy Spirit.

Type II offers help and hope to some beginning witnesses. So far, this approach appears to reproduce more trained witnesses more quickly. Spiritual multiplication may occur faster in the propositional pole. Intentionality appears to be more characteristic of Type II; and it is definitely more measurable and quantifiable than the point-of-need way.

The Typology Illuminated by Two Cases

Now, move forward with me another step. Let me give you two actual cases which will further clarify the two poles. As you read these cases, ask yourself: To which pole does this case belong and why?

"Over an Extended Period": The Case of Kathy[4]

In May of 1980 I had the privilege of baptizing four persons in one family. Ken, Jan, and their two daughters had all made commitments to Christ during our spring revival meeting. Important to note, however, is the fact that we had been vitally involved in ministry with this family for over a year. As is often the case with new Christians, this family has a number of family members and friends who are not Christians. Through my involvement with this family, I was able to meet Jan's sister, Kathy.

Kathy is twenty-six years old, divorced, and the mother of two young daughters. She has experienced a painful and chaotic life and in the last few months has found herself in a set of circumstances that have made life particularly difficult. In mid-February of 1981 I received a call from Kathy on Saturday evening asking me if I could talk with her about some problems that she had. I traveled the seventeen miles to her sister's home, where she was, and sought to be a good listener. During our time together I shared how she could gain a true foundation for her life through a personal relationship with Jesus Christ. The next week I stopped by her home to express further interest and support. I sought to respond to her needs and problems and, at the same time, offer a word of hope.

The first Monday in March I was attending a Bible study that I conduct weekly in Falls City, Nebraska. While we were having refreshments at the close of the evening's study, I received a phone call from my wife. She shared that Kathy's sister had called and I was needed there very badly. Evidently, the weight of things had really come down on Kathy and she was in a very upset state. I was thirty-five miles from her home, but made the trip as quickly as possible. As I traveled I prayed, and the Lord gave me a real sense of peace about the encounter. When I arrived Kathy was very calm. I inquired as to how I could help and the first words Kathy spoke were, "I want to accept the Lord."

I asked some questions to determine where she was in her seekings and wrestlings and felt the time was right to share how she could become a Christian. I took my New Testament and shared my own adaptation of the four spiritual laws with Kathy. Particular emphasis was given to the meaning of Christ as Lord. When I asked if she would like to pray to receive Christ as Savior and Lord, Kathy responded affirmatively and invited Jesus into her life. Since then I have sought to encourage and help Kathy as she begins her new walk with the Lord.

It is always a joy to be used as the Lord's instrument in introducing someone to Christ. As I reflect on that experience, there are some important factors that the Lord used in making me such an instrument. My contact over an extended period of time with Kathy's sister helped establish credibility. In my contact with her sister and with her, Kathy saw she could trust me. There was also the factor of availability. When need was expressed I sought to do what I could to help. I offered a Christian message but also tried to listen and respond to her problems and hurts. The Lord took all these things and used them to form a bridge Kathy could walk across to relationship with Him. May all glory and praise be His.

"On a Hill Far Away": The Case of Annie Dillard[5]

Annie Dillard in her book, *Teaching a Stone to Talk,* has a chapter entitled "On a Hill Far Away." While out on a walk beyond Tinker Creek, Dillard encountered a little boy who looked to be about eight years old. She and the boy talked about a foal who had been given to the boy by his father. Then the boy paused and looked miserably at his shoe tops. Suddenly, he lifted his corduroy cap and said in a rush, "Do you know the Lord as your personal Savior?"

Dillard replied, "Not only that, I know your mother." At that moment Annie Dillard remembered that she had visited the little boy's house one day and had been asked that same question by his mother.

About a year prior to that, Dillard had gone to the boy's house to seek permission to walk the land. She drove up a long driveway from the highway to the big house at the top of the hill. Where the driveway circled in front of the house stood an eight-foot aluminum cross with a sign beneath it which read CHRIST THE LORD IS OUR SALVATION. Around the cross in the honeysuckle were spotlights trained up at the cross and the sign.

When Dillard rang the doorbell, the woman who greeted her was nervous. She gave her permission to walk the property, provided there were "no kids . . . roughhousing." Still the lady would not let Dillard go. She was worried about something else. She wrung her hands while Dillard waited on the other side of the screen door. Then, finally, she came out with it: "Do you know the Lord as your personal Savior?"

Dillard's comments about that encounter are worth pondering:

> My heart went out to her. No wonder she had been so nervous. She must have to ask this of everyone, absolutely everyone, she meets. That is Christian witness. It makes sense, given its premises. I wanted to make her as happy as possible, reward her courage, and run.

The lady was stunned that Annie Dillard knew the Lord. She was clearly uncertain whether they were referring to the same third party. Nevertheless, she had "done her bit, bumped over the hump, and now she could relax."

Point-of-Need Type Illustrated[6]

One family was reclaimed for the Lord and His church when an adult Sunday School class met them at their points of need. This was a class of ladies with about twenty-five enrolled. Average attendance was three, two plus the teacher.

The new teacher decided that what her class needed most was intercessory prayer. Daily for one week the teacher spent an hour in prayer for class members. The next week she invited to her home the four members who attended occasionally. Then, she asked that each of them take five names from the class roll and pray for them by name every day. They were not to contact the other women, just pray for them.

One of the women for whom the teacher prayed was named Nancy. The other ladies warned their teacher: "Don't try to visit Nancy. She and her husband, Harry, are very bitter toward the church. Harry will slam the door in your face. He may insult or even hurt you."

Daily the teacher prayed for Nancy. About three weeks later one of the class members called and said Nancy was in the hospital with pneumonia. The teacher and one class member visited Nancy at the hospital. They took her some flowers.

Nancy appreciated their visit. The class member who accompanied the teacher on the visit offered to take care of Nancy's children while she was hospitalized. Nancy deeply appreciated the offer because she didn't know where else to turn. Before leaving, the two ladies left their phone numbers with Nancy in case she should need them.

The next day Nancy called the teacher to report that her husband had been unexpectedly admitted to the hospital also. He had been in an accident and injured himself. Immediately the teacher and her husband went to the hospital to meet Harry. Instead of an angry and bitter man, they found Harry more like a big, old teddy bear. He was so appreciative of the ladies' help.

When Nancy and Harry returned home from the hospital, the Sunday School class took food to them. The ladies were warmly welcomed. Nancy and Harry were so grateful that they and their two children started back to Sunday School and church. They rarely missed anything at the church after that. All they needed was for God's love to flow through God's people to them. They were won over through genuine love and concern.

The Evangelism of Jesus[7]

Jesus met persons at their points of need. He gave sight and light to the blind, acceptance and love to the outcasts, and food to the five thousand and to the four thousand.

He gave friendship to the friendless, "new wine" to the about-to-be embarrassed bridegroom, and living water to the thirsty. He gave healing to the sick, freedom to the captives, power to the powerless, cleansing to the lepers, a listening ear to inquirers, good news to the poor, joy and laughter to the weeping, and forgiveness to all sinners who sought it.

The perfect marriage between word and deed, lips and life, is seen in the model of Jesus as revealed in Scripture. Both evangelists and Christian social ministers acclaim Jesus Christ as their perfect model; the greatest hero of the evangelist and the Christian social minister is Jesus Christ.

We get the teaching about Christians being "the salt of the earth" and "the light of the world" from Jesus. Dietrich Bonhoeffer, who was hanged by Hitler shortly before the end of World War II, will forever be remembered as the theologian who called Jesus "the man for others." What Bonhoeffer actually said was that he looked upon Jesus as "one whose only concern is for others . . . man existing for others, and hence the Crucified."[8]

What does it mean to call Jesus "the man for others"? He was born for others. He came into this world to save His people from their sins. He lived His life for others. He went about doing good. He died for the sins of the world. He did not selfishly hold onto His life, but laid it down that others might live.

Jesus gave us the loving Suffering Servant model. He

taught His disciples to follow His servant example. We should be careful not to fashion our vocation of witnessing more after the image of an Amway distributor than that of the loving Suffering Servant.

Some of us seem to want only half of Christ. But as John Calvin said, "Whoever wishes to have the half of Christ, loses the whole."

Can the Christian take a stand for social justice in the name of Jesus Christ? Sherwood Eliot Wirt gave a classic answer to that question.

> The Gospels represent Jesus at times as a champion of the economically dispossessed. We see him exalting love for neighbor along with love for God. He reaches out to foreigners who are beyond the borders of the Irael of God. He seeks the release of captives, prisoners, and slaves. He denounces the scribes and religious leaders who 'devour the houses of widows.' ... His treatment of women is radically opposed to the strictures of that day. He exhibits sympathy and understanding toward children. He operates an out-patient clinic wherever he happens to be. He insists upon justice as the basis for everyday dealings between citizens ... If one summary statement of Jesus' ethics can be made, it is that love of God is best shown by love of fellow man.[9]

Jesus Christ left us a chart and compass to point the way. He gave us an example of evangelism and social involvement which we Christians can't deny.

Notes

1. For a comparable but different typology see Delos Miles, *Introduction to Evangelism* (Nashville: Broadman Press, 1983), p. 254; and Delos Miles, "Toward An Intelligent and Wholesome Evangelism," *Faith and Mission*, vol. II, no. 2, Spring 1985, p. 28.

2. See Harry F. Ward, *Social Evangelism* (New York: Missionary Education Movement of the United States and Canada, 1915). I am using the term *social evangelism* as Ward employed it to refer to the evangelism which reaches group life as well as the individual (see p. 65 esp.). See also Virginia Ramey Mollenkott, "New Age Evangelism," *Perkins Journal*, vol. XXXV, no. 2, Winter-Spring, 1982, pp. 1-7.

3. See my work referred to in note 1 for extensive references.

4. This case was written by Tommy Larner, a former student of mine at Midwestern Baptist Theological Seminary in Kansas City, Missouri, for Contemporary Evangelism 158, March 31, 1981, and is used with his permission.

5. Annie Dillard, *Teaching a Stone to Talk* (New York: Harper & Row, Publishers, 1982), pp. 77-80.

6. This story is related by W. Oscar Thompson, Jr., *Concentric Circles of Concern* (Nashville: Broadman Press, 1981), pp. 79-81. I have retold it in my own words without changing any of the facts.

7. For more on the evangelism of Jesus, see Delos Miles, *Master Principles of Evangelism* (Nashville: Broadman Press, 1982), and that book's sequel, *How Jesus Won Persons* (Nashville: Broadman Press, 1982).

8. Sherwood Eliot Wirt, *The Social Conscience of the Evangelical* (New York: Harper & Row, Publishers, 1968), pp. 21 and 158.

9. Ibid., p. 23.

10
Prophetic Evangelism

Scripture Lesson: Numbers 11:26-30; Ephesians 4:11-16

Evangelist Luis Palau said in a 1983 interview with *Christianity Today:* "I distinguish, as Ephesians 4 does, between an evangelist and a prophet. It is not my role to meddle in the prophetic."[1] Anyone who has ever been misquoted, or quoted out of context, by a news reporter can sympathize with Palau's reluctance ever again to speak off the cuff about the church and the bomb, or other potentially controversial subjects. But, sympathy and even empathy with Palau doesn't excuse such a statement. I am shocked to read that an evangelist would excuse himself from being prophetic because evangelists don't meddle.

Connecting Evangelism and Prophecy

Those evangelists who separate themselves from the Old Testament prophets either don't know or don't own their biblical heritage. They suffer an identity crisis: They don't know fully who they are or what they are about.

Nor do they pattern their ministry after Jesus Christ, the perfect model evangelist. Even the crowds knew that Jesus was the prophet from Nazareth (Matt. 21:11). They had no problem seeing Jesus in the prophetic lineage of John the Baptist, Elijah, Jeremiah, or one of the other prophets of Israel (see Matt. 16:13-14). Jesus was of course more than a prophet. Historically, the church has assigned to Jesus the offices of Prophet, Priest, and King. If the church as the body of Christ is to continue His ministry, then as the people of God we too have a prophetic, priestly, and kingly role to fill in the world. If evangelists reject their prophetic role, they refuse a role assigned to the church by Christ Himself. He sends us into the world as the Father sent Him (John 17:18; 20:21).

That neat division between prophets and evangelists, which Palau made, based on Ephesians 4:11, overlooks a number of factors. The distinction is not between New Testament evangelists and Old Testament prophets. There is not so much as a hint in the New Testament which pits New Testament evangelists against Old Testament prophets, or vice versa. Both gifts are to the church. The gifts are not mutually exclusive, and the same Christian may have two or more gifts.

I believe Palau has the gift of an evangelist. But that doesn't mean that he is the ideal model by which we define all other evangelists. An evangelist in the New Testament was a kind of pioneer missionary, an itinerant church planter. Timothy was told to "do the work of an evangelist" (2 Tim. 4:5), and Philip, one of the seven, was called "the evangelist" (Acts 21:8; 6:5). So, the only person whom the New Testament calls "the evangelist" was himself a server of tables (see Acts 6:1-7).

Where are those prophets of Ephesians 4:11 in today's church? I submit that many of them are in our pulpits and on the evangelism circuits. Among them are Palau and Billy Graham. If prophecy is more forthtelling the Word of the Lord than foretelling the future, as I believe it is, then the gift of prophecy is not dead but has been more routinized in the church's pastors and evangelists.[2]

And where are the evangelists of Ephesians 4:11 in today's church? I believe that many of them are in our pulpits and on the evangelism circuits. But even more of them are sitting in our pews every Sunday. Most of them do not know they have the gift; therefore, they are unaware of not using it.

Evangelism and prophecy, therefore, may be connected in at least three places: in the life and ministry of Jesus as our model; in the multiplicity of spiritual gifts; and in the faith-response experience of the early church. Jesus, our perfect model evangelist, practiced a prophetic evangelism. Some Christians in the early church, as in today's church, had a multiplicity of gifts. Paul, for example, was apparently endowed with several or more spiritual gifts, as are persons like Palau and Graham now. Christians such as Palau and Graham are highly visible models of one kind of prophetic evangelism, their disclaimers notwithstanding.

Furthermore, the early church duplicated the faith-response experience which characterized the faithful of ancient Israel. Among those faithful keepers of the covenant, and perhaps primarily among them, were Israel's prophets, such as Amos, Isaiah, Jeremiah, and Hosea. The same titles of privilege and responsibility ascribed to Israel in the old covenant were ascribed to the church in the new covenant (see 1 Pet. 2:9-10; Ex. 19:5-6; Isa. 43:21; Hos. 1—2). Moses' statement to Joshua, "Would that all of the Lord's people were prophets" (Num. 11:29) can now become a reality in the prophetic-evangelistic role of the new people of God, the church.

The mission assigned to the church in 1 Peter 2:9, "that you may declare the wonderful deeds of him who called you out of darkness into his marvelous light," is simultaneously prophetic and evangelistic. It is a reference to Isaiah 43:21 which says, "the people whom I formed for myself that they might declare my praise." Again, we see prophecy and evangelism joined together in the mission of the early church.

Another way of expressing this truth is through apostolic succession. Roman Catholics, Orthodox communions, and Anglicans hold to a literal and physical apostolic succession through ordination, but some of the rest of us would insist that true apostolic succession means the duplication of the faith-response experience of the apostolic church. Either way you put it, the church continues today what the twelve apostles began. The twelve continued what Jesus Christ our Lord began. And He picked up where Israel's other prophets left off. Intrinsic to apostolic succession is prophetic succession because Jesus Christ, "the apostle and high priest of our confession" (Heb. 3:1), embodied both the apostolic and prophetic traditions. That same Jesus is called "the faithful witness" (Rev. 1:5). Once more we are face to face with prophetic evangelism embodied in the Lord of the church and the Savior of the world (John 4:42).

One Model Described and Critiqued

More precisely what is this phenomenon which I have called prophetic evangelism? Let us turn to John F. Alexander for his answer. It is

> an evangelism that sounds more like Amos or Jesus than Jerry Falwell or Oral Roberts. It's an evangelism that sees the poor as victims who need to be radicalized and given self-respect as well as forgiven for their sins; they are not just a pool of cheap labor to be pacified into accepting the status quo. It's an evangelism that sees the rich as oppressors who must repent and be forgiven or face justice to come.
>
> In some cases, prophetic evangelism might look a lot like a Billy Graham rally. Except violence, greed, and racism would be denounced as clearly as sexual promiscuity and drunkenness. And coming forward would signify not only a desire to be forgiven but a willingness to fight alongside the poor.

Alexander is partial to the prophetic evangelism in which you use your body to obstruct a missile site. "Such actions become prophetic evangelism," said he, "when you make a clear statement that the nation and its people must choose between serving the crucified God and the crucifying bomb." He agrees that prophetic evangelism can also be a conversation over the back fence. "Maybe you'll be able to talk to your neighbor about God and the poor. Or maybe you'll be able to suggest that there's more to life than a new car and a secure income."

So far as I know, no other writer has described prophetic evangelism as fully as Alexander. For that reason, consider these additional statements which he makes:

> People need to be challenged to take stock of their lives. They need to explore whether they're hurting and oppressing others, whether they are committing suicide by wasting their lives, whether they are selling ice boxes on a burning deck. Then they need to be told of forgiveness through Christ's death—and of change through his resurrection.
>
> Yet many politicized Christians are hung up over evangelism. We'll vote. Or we'll march in demonstrations. Or we'll

wear badges for Solidarity and the United Farm Workers. But we hesitate to say too much about God. And we're not about to ask people whom they serve.

And that's understandable. After all, many of the most visible evangelists are peddlers of death. They are not pointing to springs of living water but to a fire escape from hell. They have preached repentance and forgiveness—but for a select list of sins. And where they've flourished, so has sexual repression, racism, legalized violence, and economic exploitation.[3]

I confess that I was profoundly moved by Alexander's provocative article; but his tone is too inflammatory; he is given to overstatement; and he has not listened as empathetically to evangelists as I should wish. More than that, he is probably too radical to work in the traditional church. So, in that respect, he speaks to us as an outsider looking in.

Nevertheless, we should take him and what he says with utmost seriousness. Why? Because there is enough truth in what he says to make us uncomfortable. His kind of prophetic evangelism is already very much on the agenda of many Christians. What Jim Wallis of the Sojourners says about "Christian conscience" looks and sounds very much like Alexander's prophetic evangelism.[4] Consider this paragraph for instance:

> Everywhere you look, Christians and churches are feeding the hungry, sheltering the homeless, ministering to the sick, organizing with the disenfranchised, visiting the prisoners, and advocating justice for the oppressed. Wherever there are works of mercy and acts of justice, Christians are in the midst of them. The faithful persistence of Christians like Dorothy Day and the *Catholic Worker* is bearing much fruit. In many places Christians are finally beginning to heed the gospel message to bring good news to the poor and the warning that we will be judged by how we treat "the least of these."[5]

Alexander's type of prophetic evangelism may pick up momentum as we move toward the next century. Among intentional Christian communities who see themselves as alternative Christian countercultures, such as Sojourners; and with an increasing number of Christians from the "old-line" denominations and Anabaptist groups, such as the Mennonites and the Bruderhof, prophetic evangelism is becoming their brand of evangelization.

Two Very Different Models

If you would prefer a very different brand of prophetic evangelism, what about that of evangelist Rudy Hernandez? This well-known Texas preacher said, "What we need today are burning prophets, coming from burning bushes, to keep sinners from a burning hell." Hernandez wasn't simply speaking of saving souls from hell in the hereafter because later on he said, "A true evangelist cannot help but see the total man, hungry in heart and mind—and in body. He has to meet man at the point of his needs."[6]

An Oklahoma pastor has found an effective method of communicating prophetic evangelism which I would label prophetic pastoral drama. Let me share that model with you.

On a recent Sunday morning, members of First Church, Kingston, Oklahoma, noticed a shabbily dressed, bearded man wandering around the church, poking in garbage cans and finally resting on the church's steps. His pants legs were worn, his cap was dirty, his shoes were old and worn, and his coat needed cleaning.

A few of them commented about "that old bum." One of the members approached the man and offered him money to buy a meal and another invited him to attend the service. *Somebody ought to have the pastor talk to him,* a few thought.

The morning service started and after the special music, much to the surprise of most of the members, the "old bum" walked in the door and started down the aisle. Some whispered, "Look there, that old guy's come inside!" Another said: "There he is . . . he's the guy who was sitting on the steps."

Not only had he come inside, he went right up to the front and walked behind the pulpit. Then he reached up and took off, first his cap and then a wig. Then Bobby Rice, Jr., told his congregation he had already delivered a sermon that morning . . . outside the church. Rice proceeded to preach his message on compassion for humanity and the sin of unconcern.

He commented on the member who had offered to buy him a meal—former Oklahoma governor Raymond Gary. After Gary's offer, Rice had revealed his identity and sworn the governor to secrecy. Next, Rice pointed out the man who invited him to church—Jim Stevenson, who was to be baptized that evening.

"I was amazed at the reactions," Rice said. "No one got mad, but they had their eyes opened to 'who is your neighbor.'" Several members told Rice later that his sermon and ruse had made them more aware of how unconcerned they are.

Keith Chronister, youth director, told Rice at the evening service he had felt guilty about not speaking to the old man and on the way home from church that morning he stopped and witnessed to two men gathering aluminum cans on the roadside.

The disguise was good enough to cause a Kingston police officer to stop Rice for questioning. The pastor had to reveal his identity to the officer and ask his cooperation.

Two young people made professions of faith during the morning service and were baptized along with four others in the evening service.

Rice used a similar technique while a member of a church in Texarkana, Arkansas. "Some of the church members there actually pushed me aside as they hurried into the church," he recalled.[7]

Values of Prophetic Evangelism

Richard Niebuhr of Yale Divinity School was asked in 1961 whether his students saw themselves as prophets or priests. "Prophets ten to one!" he replied.[8] The professor knew his students well, according to Alfred Krass who was one of them. What about today, a quarter century later?

I believe the time has come when theological students,

and many of God's people, once again want to be prophets of God. Apart from the prophetic word and vision, I see no light at the end of the tunnel of darkness through which our world is now passing. Consider with me several values of the kind of prophetic evangelism to which I have been pointing.

Prophetic evangelism is an evangelism of repentance. One of those recapitulatory passages in Mark's Gospel sums up our Lord's preaching in these words: "Now after John was arrested, Jesus came into Galilee, preaching the gospel of God, and saying, 'The time is fulfilled, and the kingdom of God is at hand; repent, and believe in the gospel' " (Mark 1:14-15). John the Baptist came preaching "a baptism of repentance for the forgiveness of sins" (Mark 1:4). God told the people of Israel through His prophet Ezekiel: "Repent and turn from all your transgressions, lest iniquity be your ruin" (Ezek. 18:30). Paul in the middle of the Areopagus told the Greek intellectuals: "God . . . commands all men everywhere to repent" (Acts 17:30). Beyond doubt, both the prophetic and apostolic traditions called for everybody to turn from their sins and to God.

The repentance called for in prophetic evangelism is from both personal and social sins. As a matter of fact, I can't find two separate lists of sins in the Bible, one which we might label personal and another social. The Bible has no narrow lists of sins. Its conception of evil is broad and biting. And that's one of the things which makes evangelism biblical and prophetic.

Jeremiah in one of his sermons condemned adultery and coveting a neighbor's wife: "They committed adultery and trooped to the houses of harlots. They were well-fed lusty stallions, each neighing for his neighbor's wife" (Jer. 5:7-8). Later in that same message, Jeremiah said:

> The house of Israel and the house of Judah have been utterly faithless to me . . . They set a trap; they catch men. Like a basket full of birds, their houses are full of treachery; therefore, they have become great and rich, they have grown fat and sleek. They know no bounds in deeds of wickedness; they judge not with justice the cause of the fatherless, to make it

prosper, and they do not defend the rights of the needy (vv. 11, 26-28).

If we practice prophetic evangelism, we shall call all persons, including ourselves, to turn from their wicked ways. We shall condemn economic oppression as strongly as we do rape. God never intended that we grow fat and sleek while kids starve. Stealing persons' dignity is as bad as armed robbery. Prophetic evangelism tells persons they don't have to get rich or get even in order to have the good life; what they have to do is repent of their sins and turn to God, the fountain of all life. Either we repent or we perish!

Prophetic evangelism calls us to a consistent pro-life ethic. It vigorously opposes abortion on demand, but at the same time it calls for a defense of human life wherever it is threatened. Therefore, it rejects the selective morality of both the "right" and the "left" and weaves into a "seamless garment" issues such as the right to life, capital punishment, war and peace, nuclear weapons, defense of the poor, and the pursuit of economic justice for all.

Prophetic evangelism can help us rid ourselves of gnostic tendencies. Like the heretical Gnostics who plagued the early church, there is a tendency among us to denigrate the physical world and to spiritualize everything. They denied that Jesus Christ had come in the flesh (see 1 John 4: 2-3). Some of them went so far as to say that Jesus left no footprints as He walked on the wet, sandy beach. Matter to them was evil. They had an inadequate doctrine of creation.

Some of us, like Marcion, want to write our own Bible and leave out the Old Testament. We are strong on the divinity of Jesus Christ, but weak on His full humanity. We sometimes call ourselves "New Testament Christians," as though the Old Testament were not also a part of the canon. It is that kind of neognosticism which prophetic evangelism can destroy. Prophetic evangelism insists that we have an adequate doctrine of creation to accompany our doctrine of the new creation. It will not permit us to call evil what God called "very good" (Gen. 1:31).

Prophetic evangelism constructs a theological bridge between evangelism and social involvement. It puts New Testament saints in communion with Old Testament saints. It tells the whole story of God's mighty acts and does not shortchange the biblical revelation.

Notes

1. "Luis Palau: Evangelist to Three Worlds," *Christianity Today*, vol. 27, no. 9, May 20, 1983, p. 32.
2. I acknowledge that all prophecy has not been routinized in today's church. But when I have seen what some may call "spontaneous" expressions of prophecy in Pentecostal and neo-Pentecostal settings, even that was circumscribed into what I would call a routine.
3. John F. Alexander, "Prophetic Evangelism," *The Other Side*, issue 141, vol. 19, no. 6, June, 1983, p. 8.
4. Jim Wallis, "The Rise of Christian Conscience," *Sojourners*, vol. 14, no. 1, January, 1985, pp. 12-16.
5. *Ibid.*, p. 15.
6. Phyllis Thompson, "Rudy Hernandez: the Only Thing He Loves More Than Preaching Is People," *Missions USA*, vol. 56, no. 3, 1985, p. 17.
7. I am indebted to Bob E. Matthews, associate editor of the *Baptist Messenger* for permission to use this story exactly as he wrote it. It appeared as " 'Bum' Opens Eyes to Needy," in the *Religious Herald*, vol. CLVIII, no. 19, May 16, 1985, p. 24.
8. Alfred Krass, "Rules for Prophets: A Pastoral Way to Work for Justice," *The Other Side*, vol. 21, no. 2, issue 161, March 1985, p. 78.

11
Advice for Christian Social Ministers and Evangelists

Scripture Lesson: Isaiah 44:3; 1 Corinthians 12:14-26

F. Scott Fitzgerald, in his novel *The Crack Up,* described the test of a first-rate intelligence as "the ability to hold two opposing ideas in the mind at the same time." I do not see evangelism and social involvement as opposing ideas. However, as we have already seen, some do; and that's another reason for this chapter.

What I have to say will, I hope, be applicable to all of God's people who are engaged in social ministry and/or evangelism. But I address my advice in particular to professional Christian social ministers and evangelists. My heart's desire is to gain wider acceptance for both.

Advice to Christian Social Ministers

Resist the Temptation to Throw Cold Water

You may be tempted to dash cold water in the faces of certain practitioners of evangelism. But resist that evil impulse. Even if they don't do like you think they should, rejoice over their concern for persons. God has not called any of us to go around throwing cold water on other Christians—not even upon those whose evangelistic methodology may be personally obnoxious to us.

The beloved disciple, John, on one occasion told Jesus: "Master, we saw a man casting out demons in your name, and we forbade him, because he does not follow with us" (Luke 9:49). Jesus said to John, "Do not forbid him; for he that is not against you is for you" (v. 50).

Christian social workers are bombarded with so many human needs that they may be tempted to disparage their brothers and sisters in Christ who seem to be concerned only with the souls of individuals. If so, beware. Where those witnesses are, some of us once were. Had you not rather see spiritual needs met than no needs at all? Besides, do we not have biblical precedents for dealing with "weaker" members of the family of God (see 1 Cor. 9:22; 10:23 to 11:1; Rom. 14:1 to 15:6)?

If you perceive yourself to be strong in the faith, then you are under obligation to welcome the one who is weak (Rom. 14:1; 15:7). Our Lord's example teaches us not to go around breaking bruised reeds and snuffing out smoldering wicks (Matt. 12:20). We are to welcome one another as Christ has welcomed us (Rom. 15:7).

Make Peace with Your Heritage

Back in the early 1970s, I was in a world mission conference. An assortment of missionaries had come from home and abroad to share about their ministries with a group of churches. One of those missionaries was a Christian social minister who was so different from the rest of us that the churches refused to hear him. It grieved me that, because feelings against his outspokenness ran so high, the leaders sent him back home before the conference ended.

As I reflect on that embarrassing experience, I have concluded that even though the social minister was right in his facts he may have been wrong in his attitude. He spoke the truth, but perhaps he did not speak it with enough *agapē*. His style was so abrasive, insensitive, and belligerent that he was obnoxious to the very people whom he wanted to change. It was as though he had a chip on his shoulder.

Having listened to him speak and spent some time conversing with him, I perceived that he had never made peace with his denominational heritage. I could empathize with him because I had once stood out like a sore thumb myself in similar situations. There must have been times when churches wanted to send me back home before the time was up. I know there were some times when I wanted to go back home before I was through. But by the grace of God, and because they were more mature in Christ than I, I didn't and they didn't.

If you can't make peace with your denominational heritage, whatever it is, you will have a difficult time as a Christian social minister. Especially is that true if you belong to a communion which tends to be suspicious of social ministers. You don't have to sell your soul, but you do have to "pay your rent."

Somewhere in his book *Structures of Prejudice*, Carlyle Marney said something which helped me along those lines. The gist of it was: I am not about to exchange one set of walls for another set of walls, especially when the other set is taller, thicker, and closer together. So far, outside of my Southern Baptist heritage, I haven't found another set of walls which afford me as much freedom.

That's what I mean by making peace with your heritage. Don't take a salary from a church or denomination you don't love. If *evangelism* is a dirty word for you as a social minister and those who pay your salary expect you to be evangelistic, but in good conscience you feel you can't, either get yourself a wholesome and intelligent evangelism or find yourself some other place of service.

Keep People Scratching

Sojourner Truth was a slave woman who could neither read nor write. But she never gave up talking and fighting against slavery or second-class treatment of women. A heckler once told Sojourner that he cared no more for her antislavery talk "than for a flea bite." Sojourner answered, "Maybe not, but the Lord willing, I'll keep you scratching."[1] You may be few or even one. Nevertheless, you can keep those people scratching who would turn a deaf ear to issues of justice and peace.

Even if you can't go around throwing cold water on enthusiastic soul winners, and although you have to make some kind of truce with your heritage, that shouldn't neuter or silence you. Your prophetic function remains. One of Martin Luther's sayings was: "The fact of being a public preacher commits me to exhort a man if, seduced by the devil, he is not able to see what he is doing as injustice."[2]

You can be proactive rather than reactive. God's compassion for all persons is a part of authentic evangelism. That's what the Book of Jonah is all about. God loves all persons, all races, children, men, and women.

One of my former white students, as a boy growing up in Baltimore, Maryland, invited a black boy to come into his church. An adult standing by said, "What are you doing, Mark?" Mark answered, "I'm letting my friend into the church building." The adult said, "He doesn't belong here." Mark never has forgotten that. He is a United Methodist minister today. And Mark is still inviting all people into our Lord's church. That's one of the things you can do to keep people scratching.

Jackie Robinson, a generation ago, was the first black man to play major league baseball. He found himself facing constant racial harrassment. One day during a Brooklyn Dodgers game in Cincinnati, when the racial taunts from the crowd reached a crescendo, a white teammate, Pee Wee Reese, called time out. Slowly, Reese walked over to Robinson, put his arm around his shoulder and stood there for a long moment, eloquently and wordlessly telling the crowd: This is my friend.[3] That's one kind of prophetic scratching you can do even without words.

Don't Get Callouses on Your Heart

Lee Kuan Yew, the prime minister of Singapore, speaking of his decision not to allow Vietnamese boat refugees to land in his country, said: "You have to develop callouses on your heart; otherwise you will bleed to death."[4] I don't believe that for a moment.

You may be tempted to get callouses on your heart, but guard against that temptation with all your might and with the might of God's Spirit.

Remember Kitty Genovese? On March 13, 1964 Catherine (Kitty) Genovese, a twenty-eight-year-old bar manager, was stalked and stabbed to death in her Queens neighborhood of New York City. Her cries for help went unanswered by thirty-eight of her neighbors. Again and again, the killer stalked and stabbed her for more than half an hour.[5]

Why did Miss Genovese's neighbors not come to her rescue, or at the least call the police? Was it because of the late hour of 3:20 to 3:50 AM? Did they think it was just a lover's quarrel? Were they afraid? Were they too tired? Did they not know what to do? Or, were they apathetic and simply didn't want to get involved? Did they have callouses on their heart?

Kitty Genovese was heard to say, "Oh, my God, he stabbed me." She screamed out, "Please help me!" Windows opened and lights went on in the building across the street. One man yelled down from the seventh floor, "Let that girl alone." Yet, nobody went to her aid.

Are we flecks of dust floating around in a vacuum? Or, are we our brothers' and sisters' keepers?

I do not bring up the case of Kitty Genovese in order to condemn her neighbors. Certainly my purpose is not to add to the antiurban sentiment which abounds in our society.

However, I would suggest that this case is a parable which gives us one picture of the kind of persons and structures we are called to evangelize and serve. Our country is not overflowing with good Samaritans. There are many victims, or many Catherine Genoveses as it were. We also have our share of Winston Moseleys, or persons like the confessed and convicted murderer of Genovese who set out "to rape and rob and to kill a girl." Then, too, there are those thirty-eight witnesses who did not get involved.

If we get callouses on our hearts, we shall become more like the thirty-eight witnesses in that tragedy than like the witnesses in the early church. You see so much need, encounter so many victims so often, and experience so many obstacles. But, whatever you do, don't get callouses on your heart.

Advice to Evangelists

Avoid the Superchurch-Superpastor Trap

Christians and churches may be measured by their commitment to the least, the lost, and the last, but not by size. Those of us who have committed our lives to evangelistic ministries tend to fall into the trap of measuring churches by the three B's of baptisms, buildings, and budgets. We, unwittingly I think, give the impression that the churches and pastors who baptize the most people annually are the really great churches of America and the world. That's the reason some of our critics accuse us of being afflicted with numerical neurosis. This is the kind of thing which turns Christian social ministers off.

We need to really work at avoiding the superchurch-superpastor trap. We can properly affirm the superchurches and their pastors without giving the impression that they are the ideal models after which all should pattern. Prosperity—even institutional church prosperity—without concern for biblical justice, unambiguously signifies disobedience.

We may say that we don't have a superchurch complex, but do the facts deny our statement? We are more conditioned by the ethos of our culture than some of us have imagined. Our culture asserts that "bigger is better" and seems to be enamored by the myth of unlimited growth. But by what logic do we invite a superchurch pastor to be the featured speaker at a small-church conference?

If we would abstain from all appearances of evil in this matter, at least two avenues are open to us. Those of us who work full time in evangelism and are responsible for planning programs can invite preachers to speak at our meetings who represent a larger variety of pastoral role models. Even if we feel strong affinity with the superaggressive pastors, we are servants of all the people of God, and therefore, have no right to propagandize persons with our personal points of view. As we give visibility and legitimacy to other pastors and speakers, along with the superchurch pastors, our critics will know that we are not playing some numbers game with human beings.

That first avenue will bring almost immediate results in improved relations with our colleagues in Christian social ministries. The second avenue will be more long term, but may produce more lasting fruit. We have to learn how to make evangelism the center of our concern but not its circumference.

Let me see if I can clarify that. American Baptist Churches (ABC) held a National Convocation on Evangelism in 1981. This was the first national conference devoted entirely to evangelism in the history of the denomination. Some 900 persons registered, with as many as 1,800 attending evening rallies. Emmett V. Johnson, national director of evangelism for the ABC, said he foresaw "a new day" for evangelism in the ABC. "Evangelism will be the center of our concern but not its circumference," said Johnson. "We're not so much interested in winning souls as in making disciples who will affect our world and win others to Christ."[6]

So long as evangelism is both the center and circumference of our concern, we run the risk of falling into the superchurch-superpastor trap. The ultimate goal of evangelism should be the kingdom of God, not church growth and not some form of Godliness without the power of God flowing through that form.

Don't Confuse Orthodoxy with Evangelism

Evangelism should not be confused with orthodoxy. Some of the most unevangelistic persons in the church are some of the most orthodox. Somewhere along the way we began to identify evangelism with orthodoxy and social ministry with unorthodoxy. Both conclusions are patently false and should be jettisoned immediately. Careless practices like that could cause us to libel some faithful servants of God.

The Book of James says, "You believe that God is one; you do well. Even the demons believe—and shudder" (2:19). Those who automatically jump to the conclusion that if you believe the right doctrines you are evangelistic are shallow and naive. The demons believe and shudder at the truths they believe, yet they remain unclean and unconverted demons.

Alan Walker, an Australian Methodist, told a Methodist Conference in South Africa that "there is no greater menace in the church than a born-again Christian without a social conscience." That kind of preaching up and down South Africa in 1980 resulted in Walker being told by the state to pack his bags and go back to Australia.[7]

What Walker said in the context of South African apartheid may have been true. Our problem in America, however, is not only born-again Christians without social consciences but also born-again Christians without evangelistic concern. To me, born-again orthodox Christians who believe the right doctrines but who have no evangelistic conscience are just as great, if not greater, a menace to the church.

My advice to evangelistic co-workers is to be better fruit inspectors. Don't confuse orthodoxy either with evangelism or with Christian social ministry. Orthopraxy is the final proof of orthodoxy (see Matt. 7:15-23).

See Social Ministries Establishing Credibility

Christian social ministries can open doors to witnessing opportunities. They may establish credibility so essential to effective evangelism. Many years ago, when Dr. Kenneth Chafin was the evangelism leader for Southern Baptists, he said something I hope never to forget: "Evangelism moves forward best on the wings of ministry." If you want your evangelism to fly, couple it with authentic ministries which meet the needs of human beings.

Take a ministry as unglamorous as child care for example. First Baptist Church, Papillion, Nebraska, established more credibility through its Weekday Early Education program than through any other method. John B. Cox, who was pastor of that congregation in 1981, told me that nothing which his church was doing had brought them the kind of acceptance in the community as their WEE school for three- and four-year-olds.

No accurate figures are available, but we can conservatively estimate that approximately 40 percent of all child care in the United States takes place in churches. Many parents are anxious to find churches which offer quality care for their children.

Literacy ministry would be another good example. Literacy evangelism may be one of the best means for evangelizing the underprivileged. Almost half of the world can't read.

Yet, 99 percent of the world's people have some Scripture printed in their language.[8]

It is high time for us evangelists to see that we have to *serve* the gospel as well as share it verbally. If we can see Christian social ministers as those who help establish credibility for sharing the gospel through their serving of it, world evangelization will be blessed by our vision. Tomorrow's society may be totally secular. Only a ministering church will get through to it.

Advice to Both

Model What You Believe

The best advice I can give to evangelists and Christian social ministers is to model what you believe. When someone has seen the love of God acted out, it is easier to believe. It authenticates the gospel to outsiders, inquirers, and church members.

Many years ago W. H. Lax pastored a church in a poor section of London. Learning that a man who claimed no faith was gravely ill, he went to visit him. The man wouldn't say a word and made it clear the preacher was not welcome. Noting the sparsity of food in the house, Lax stopped at a butcher shop on the way home and had two lamb chops sent to the man. There was better response on the next visit. Again, he sent two chops. This went on until he was greeted warmly, allowed to read Scripture, and pray. Later Lax returned from a visit out of the city and was told the man had died, but had left a message: "Tell Mr. Lax it's all right. I'm going to God. But be sure to tell him that it wasn't his preaching that saved me. It was those lamb chops."[9]

I toured the newly commissioned *USS Nicholas* in 1984 and met a chief petty officer who had been in the U. S. Navy thirty-eight years. He said to us, "I am not *in* the Navy; I *am* the Navy!" Are you the living bridge between evangelism and social involvement? There is no better way to close this gap than to stand in it yourself.

A final word on modeling is that you will be wise to follow

the Jesus model. "No. 1 Jesus Man." How is that for a title? That was the title given Pope John Paul II in Papua, New Guinea, by tribal warriers and grass-skirted women in pidgin English, whose ancestors routinely cannabalized nineteenth-century Christian missionaries.

In pidgin English or whatever language, that title communicates something about Jesus as the model. Jesus modeled perfect proportion, beautiful balance, and sweet symmetry between evangelism and social involvement. One verse of Scripture has Him teaching, preaching, and healing in the same sentence (see Matt. 9:35).

Be Realistic About Change

We may never take the whole church with us in evangelism or social involvement. If we wait until all go with us, we shall never go anywhere, do anything, or accomplish much. The only encouraging word to be said about that realistic appraisal is that "little is much" when it comes to the work of evangelism and social involvement. One truly committed person can move mountains in partnership with God.

So far as I know, no one ever accused Dorothy Day of not being a change agent. I was born in the same year (1933) that Day published her first issue of the *Catholic Worker*. This monthly social justice paper had a circulation around 100,000 in 1983. One of Day's favorite quotations from William James was:

> I am done with great things and big things, great institutions and big success, and I am for those tiny invisible molecular moral forces that work from individual to individual, creeping through the crannies of the world like so many rootlets, or like the capillary oozing of water, yet which, if you give them time, will rend the hardest monuments of man's pride.[10]

Some of the really effective institutions for change in our society are but extensions of the shadow of one person or a couple or a small group. Day's work is but one example. I believe Voice of Calvary is such an example. Sojourners in

Washington, D. C., and Jubilee in Philadelphia could also be mentioned.

Let us not think that our grandiose schemes will change the world. There is no easy fix of any kind for the social, moral, and religious problems of our society. On the other hand, let us not think for a moment that we can't make a difference. Our problems are not unsolvable. There is hope and there is help in God.

Three things I know for certain about change in the free church tradition are: It comes slowly and in small increments; we have to be content with small gains; and we are change agents for God. Beyond that I believe no good done in the name of Christ will ever be lost. Our business is to "work the works of him who sent" us, "while it is day; night comes, when no one can work" (John 9:4).

Affirm Each Other

We keep wanting to be separate grains and separate grapes in the common loaf of bread and the common cup. But until each grain is crushed and ground up, it is not truly a part of the common loaf. And until each grape is crushed with the other grapes, it cannot be a part of the common cup of the Lord.

When one makes a circle with a compass, the larger the circle, the more firmly the compass needs to be placed in the center. Likewise, the more we reach out in ministry, the deeper our relationships with Christ and one another need to be. None of us can lose himself or herself so completely in evangelism or social involvement that he or she no longer needs to relate to Christ or to other Christians. On the contrary, the more we reach out to the world, the greater we need to reach inward toward Christ and the Christian community.

The church may be compared to a lantern which has a bright and shining light in it. That light shines out through the lantern glass to all the world. Think of the rays of light as brothers and sisters sent out on mission. Those messengers sent out are not independent. Nor do they undertake anything on their own. Also, the church community is not shut in on itself and does not undertake anything for its own sake. The nature of the church is to shine, to send out light.

One thing all of us can and should do is affirm each other. The body of Christ is incomplete without us all. Apart from evangelism, the church will die. Without social involvement, the love of God does not abide in her. Without both, we have a truncated gospel out of balance and out of tune.

Conclusion

We should be able to affirm our brothers and sisters in the body of Christ who believe strongly in social justice. Some are willing to go to jail for their witness. The Philippian jailer and his household were saved when Paul and Silas were jailed for engaging in evangelization and social involvement in Philippi (see Acts 16:16-39).

Many Christians today seek to combine evangelism and social involvement as Paul and Silas did. Ken Medema, a popular evangelistic musician, has sought to become a living bridge across the troubled waters of evangelism and social involvement. Medema tells how he and other Christians were able to witness to secular peace activists after they were arrested in 1982 for peacefully demonstrating at a nuclear-weapons research plant in Livermore, California. In jail all the men were given little packets containing a toothbrush, a tube of toothpaste, a bar of soap, a washcloth, and a Bible. Some of the guys made fun of the Bible. But Medema and the other Christians said to them, "Do you realize that this Bible is the reason we're here?" They proceeded to show how their jail experience came out of their biblical faith. That was an evangelistic experience for many of the men.[11]

Notes

1. Marian Wright Edelman, "In Defense of Children," *Light*, September, 1983, p. 7. Published by the Christian Life Commission of the SBC.

2. Cited by Philip Potter, "Faith, Church and Society: Luther's Ecumenical Heritage," *One World*, no. 90, October-November 1983, p. 31.

Advice for Christian Social Ministers and Evangelists

3. See Judy Foreman, "Friend Also May be Lifesaver, Social Scientists Say," *The News and Observer*, Raleigh, NC, March 25, 1982, p. 21A.

4. Quoted by Stan Mooneyham, "How to Avoid Compassion Burn-out," *Seeds*, vol. 6, no. 8, August 1983, p. 9.

5. For fuller information, see Maureen Dowd, "20 Years after Kitty Genovese's Murder, Experts Study Bad Samaritanism," and "The Night that 38 Stood By as a Life Was Lost," *The New York Times*, March 12, 1984, p. 15.

6. See "American Baptists Ring the Evangelism Gong," *Christianity Today*, XXV, no. 4, February 20, 1981, p. 42.

7. See "Evangelist Banned," *The Christian Century*, vol. XCVII, no. 37, November 19, 1980, p. 1121.

8. See Robert Rice, "Imprisoned in Mind and Soul," *Global Church Growth*, vol. XIX, no. 5, September-October, 1982, pp. 212-214.

9. Don Rose, an associate pastor of First Baptist Church, Greenville, S. C., called this a "true story." *The News*, Vol. XXVI, No. 7, February 15, 1984, p. 3. Published by First Baptist Church, Greenville, S. C.

10. Cited by Nancy L. Roberts, "The *'Catholic Worker'*: 50 Years of Fortitude," *The Christian Century*, vol. 100, no. 12, April 27, 1983, p. 391.

11. Related in Kathleen Hayes's interview with Ken Medema, "Media Focus, Ken Medema: Storytelling Evangelist," *The Other Side*, vol. 21, no. 4, issue 163, June 1985, p. 57.

Annotated Bibliography

Anderson, Gerald H. ed. *Witnessing to the Kingdom: Melbourne and Beyond* (Maryknoll, N.Y.: Orbis Books, 1982). 170 pp.

Contains the official report of the Conference on World Mission and Evangelism, meeting in Melbourne, Australia, May 12-24, 1980 and sponsored by the Commission on World Mission and Evangelism of the World Council of Churches (pp. 105-167); a chapter by Philip Potter putting the conference in historical perspective; and responses to the Melbourne document by an evangelical leader, a Roman Catholic, a Greek Orthodox, etc.

Arias, Mortimer. *Announcing the Reign of God: Evangelization and the Subversive Memory of Jesus* (Philadelphia: Fortress Press, 1984). 155 pp.

Arias, a former bishop of the Methodist Church in Bolivia, presents a kingdom approach to evangelism as a meeting point between evangelization and Christian social ethics. He lifts up Jesus Christ, "the first evangelist of the kingdom," as a model.

Armstrong, James. *From the Underside: Evangelism from a Third World Vantage Point* (Maryknoll, N.Y.: Orbis Books, 1981). 93 pp.

A fresh approach to evangelism by a former bishop in the United Methodist Church. Armstrong contends that "Spheres of influence, structures, and institutions need to be evangelized as truly as the habits, attitudes, and lifestyles of the individual" (p. 25).

Arnold, Eberhard. *A Testimony of Church Community from His Life and Writings* (Rifton, N. Y.: Plough Publishing House, 1973 ed.). 107 pp.

Arnold founded the original Bruderhof Community in Germany in 1920. These words summarize the faith and hope which has guided the Bruderhof Communities. The book can help us understand the intentional Christian community approach to evangelism and social involvement.

Barreiro, Alvaro. *Basic Ecclesial Communities: The Evangelization of the Poor.* Translated from Portuguese by Barbara Campbell (Maryknoll, N. Y.: Orbis Books, 1982). 82 pp.

The basic ecclesial communities of Latin America present a new, and primarily Roman Catholic, model for linking evangelism and social involvement. This is a kingdom-oriented, liberation approach which some are now attempting to duplicate in America.

Annotated Bibliography

Bennett, G. Willis. *Effective Urban Church Ministry* (Nashville: Broadman Press, 1983). 180 pp.

Based on a thorough case study of Allen Temple Baptist Church, a predominantly black congregation in Oakland, California, dually aligned with the Progressive National Baptist Convention and the American Baptist Convention, USA. Depicts a dynamic church which models the bridging of evangelism and social involvement.

Bennett, John C. ed. *Christian Social Ethics in a Changing World* (New York: Association Press, 1966). 381 pp.

An ecumenical inquiry into the theological problems of social ethics, by twenty Christian scholars from around the world, under the auspices of the World Council of Churches.

Biéler, André. *The Social Humanism of Calvin.* Translated by Paul T. Fuhrmann (Richmond, Va.: John Knox Press, 1964). 79 pp.

Original French edition was 1961. The monograph is based on a much larger and fully documented volume by Bieler entitled *The Economic and Social Thought of Calvin.* Biéler gives a summary of the central convictions of Calvin on money, wealth and property. He reveals a Calvin often not seen through Calvinism and Puritanism, and very different than the current image of him as the father of laissez faire capitalism. Glimpses of Calvin's social involvement through a social medical service and relief for the needy (pp. 38-39) may be seen.

Bockmuehl, Klaus. *Evangelicals and Social Ethics*, no. 4 in "Outreach and Identity: Evangelical Theological Monographs," for the World Evangelical Fellowship Theological Commission, translated by David T. Priestly (Downers Grove, Ill.: Inter Varsity Press, 1975). 47 pp.

Accurately subtitled, "A Commentary on Article 5 of the Lausanne Covenant." Discusses and critiques the three major lectures on social ethics given to the International Congress on World Evangelization in Lausanne in 1974 by Rene Padilla, Samuel Escobar, and Carl F. H. Henry. Bockmuehl offers a strong biblically based commentary on the nine verbs of action in article 5 which treats the social responsibility of Christians.

Bosch, David J. *Witness to the World: The Christian Mission in Theological Perspective* (Atlanta: John Knox Press, 1980). 277 pp.

The brilliant missiologist from South Africa does not give us another introduction to missiology. His focus is on the *theology* of mission. Mission, he sees as more comprehensive than evangelism (p. 15), but both have to do with the crossing of frontiers.

Briggs, Bill. *Faith Through Works: Church Renewal Through Mission* (Franconia, N. H.: Thorn Books, Inc., 1983). 93 pp.

Briggs shares his failure in Chicago and Buffalo and his success in Franconia, New Hampshire. If the Franconia Church of Christ, in a town with 752 population, can be renewed through mission, there is hope for other churches. Read it as a parable to teach how one local church has put evangelism and social involvement together.

Campolo, Anthony. *Ideas for Social Action* (El Cajon, Calif.: Youth Specialties, 1983). 162 pp.

A handbook on mission and service for young people, biblically based, challenging, simple, and practical—right down to the mailing addresses you need.

Castro, Emilio. *Sent Free: Mission and Unity in the Perspective of the Kingdom* (Grand Rapids: William B. Eerdmans Publishing Co., 1985). 102 pp.

The general secretary of the World Council of Churches argues that the mission of the church is the mission of the kingdom of God, not church growth, or the evangelization of the world in our time, or Christian presence, or humanization. He tries to convince us that only the perspective of the kingdom is broad enough and biblical enough to bring Christians together in unity and to send them out on mission in freedom.

Cole, Jr., Charles C. *The Social Ideas of the Northern Evangelists 1826-1860* (New York: Octagon Books, Inc., 1966). 268 pp.

Originally published in 1954 by Columbia University Press. Cole's book came out three years before Timothy Smith's revolutionary *Revivalism and Social Reform* (1957), and reached a very different conclusion. It is a study of "the secular ideas of the Northern evangelists during the years 1826-1860 (p. 3), which attempts to evaluate their influence on American social and intellectual development. Those who want to get in touch with their nineteenth-century evangelical roots in evangelism and social ethics will find here some rich ore to be mined.

Conn, Harvie M. *Evangelism: Doing Justice and Preaching Grace* (Grand Rapids: Zondervan Publishing House, 1982). 112 pp.

Conn is professor of missions at Westminster Theological Seminary in Philadelphia. This is not another exercise in blackboard evangelism. Conn opts for wholistic, Lordship evangelism done in context, which shows and tells mercy and grace. He tells of his discovery that persons are sinned against as well as sinners.

Costas, Orlando E. *Christ Outside the Gate: Mission Beyond Christendom* (Maryknoll, N.Y.: Orbis Books, 1982). 238 pp.

Costas, now Dean of the Faculty at Andover Newton Theological School, gives us what one reviewer called "the most succinct, yet comprehensive analysis of the missiological issues facing the church and the churches that has appeared in many years." Costas writes from the background of a Hispanic evangelical, but he manages to keep one foot firmly planted in the ecumenical camp (Geneva) and the other in the evangelical camp (Lausanne). There is much grist here for the theological mill which tries to produce a wholesome and intelligent evangelism mixed with Christocentric social involvement.

Annotated Bibliography

Dayton, Donald W. *Discovering an Evangelical Heritage* (New York: Harper & Row, Publishers, 1976). 147 pp.

Dayton shares his own struggle to find an evangelical identity in the 1960s and 70s. The book is an historical overview of nineteenth-century evangelical reformers such as Jonathan Blanchard, Charles G. Finney, Theodore Weld, Catherine Booth, and the Tappan brothers (Lewis and Arthur). The author also treats the role of evangelical institutions like Oberlin and Wheaton. His chapter 10, "Whatever Happened to Evangelicalism?" is the best explanation I have read for what Smith and Moberg called "the Great Reversal."

Dayton Edward R. and Wilson, Samuel, eds. *The Future of World Evangelization* (Monrovia, Calif. Missions Advanced Research and Communication Center, 1984). 717 pp.

A volume in MARC's "Unreached Peoples" series. Looks back on the past ten years since the 1974 International Congress on World Evangelization at Lausanne, Switzerland, and looks forward to the next ten years. Reveals from an evangelical point of view the increasing linkages between world evangelization and social involvement. A shorter edition (277 pp.) of the same book is available without the listings of the unreached peoples.

Dryness, William A. *Let the Earth Rejoice: A Biblical Theology of Holistic Mission* (Westchester, Ill. Crossway Books, 1983). 216 pp.

An inquiry into whether there is a biblical warrant for seeing a political and social dimension to mission and evangelism. Attempts to answer the question: What is the biblical view of God's mission in the world? A substantive biblical theology of mission.

Dyck, Cornelius J. *Witness and Service in North America* (Scottdale, Penn.: Herald Press, 1980), 122 pp.

This is volume 3 of selected Mennonite Central Committee documents highlighting MCC involvements in North America. Forty-nine readings are selected and contextualized relating to peace, Mennonite Mental Health Services (MMHS), Voluntary Service, and Mennonite Disaster Service (MDS). MDS began with a Sunday School picnic in 1950 and has touched thousands of lives suffering the ravages of tornadoes, floods, earthquakes, and other disasters.

Eighmy, John Lee. *Churches in Cultural Captivity* (Knoxville: The University of Tennessee Press, 1972). 250 pp.

Subtitled, "A History of the Social Attitudes of Southern Baptists." Carefully documented work. Shows that Southern Baptists for sixty years "assumed the role of a cultural establishment by sanctifying a secular order devoted to states' rights, white supremacy, laissez faire economics, and property rights." Eighmy convincingly argues that the social gospel did have a direct influence on Southern Baptists, destroying the uniformity of their nineteenth-century social thought and creating two opposing interpretations of the church's mission, one of them individualistic and the other corporate. An aggressive program of evangelism is coordinated with church democracy to account for the social record of Southern Baptists.

Escobar, Samuel and Driver, John. *Christian Mission and Social Justice* (Scottdale, Penn.: Herald Press, 1978). 112 pp.

This is Missionary Studies No. 5 in a series sponsored by the Institute of Mennonite Studies, Elkhart, Indiana. R. Pierce Beaver, now retired from The Divinity School of the University of Chicago, writes the introduction. Escobar of Peru does three of the chapters. Driver was formerly a Mennonite missionary in Uruguay. All three writers are conscious of the overlapping of evangelism and social involvement.

Evangelism in Reformed Perspective: An Evangelism Manifesto (Grand Rapids: The Church Herald, Inc., 1977). 16 pp.

A joint declaration on evangelism from the Reformed perspective prepared by the Reformed Church in America and the Christian Reformed Church. Strong on the kingdom of God motif. Available from 1324 Lake Drive, S. E., Grand Rapids, MI 49506.

Galilea, Segundo. *The Beatitudes: To Evangelize as Jesus Did.* Translated from Spanish by Robert R. Barr (Maryknoll, N.Y.: Orbis Books, 1984). 108 pp.

Galilea is a Roman Catholic priest in Santiago, Chile. His thesis is that "The Beatitudes show us evangelization through the eyes of Jesus" (p. 10). Lifts up Christ as "the Evangelizer" whom all Christians are to imitate.

Gallardo, José. *The Way of Biblical Justice* (Scottdale, Penn.: Herald Press, 1983). 76 pp.

An Anabaptist-Mennonite perspective on justice, by a Mennonite scholar who was born and reared as a Roman Catholic in Spain. Gallardo shows that biblical justice goes beyond human justice and beyond law; that it includes concepts of well-being, wholeness, righteousness, and peace. This is volume 11 in the Mennonite Faith Series.

Grand Rapids Report—Evangelism and Social Responsibility: An Evangelical Commitment. Lausanne Occasional Papers No. 21 (Published by the Lausanne Committee for World Evangelization and the World Evangelical Fellowship, 1982). 64 pp.

This is the official report of the international Consultation on the Relationship between Evangelism and Social Responsibility, held at Grand Rapids, Michigan, June 19-25, 1982. The consultation was jointly sponsored by the Lausanne Committee and WEF. John Stott was responsible for the final editing. Called, "Evangelism and Social Responsibility," the report is the most definitive statement on the relationship between the two ambits that we have from evangelicals.

Greenway, Roger S. *Calling Our Cities to Christ* (Nutley, N. J.: Presbyterian and Reformed Publishing Co., 1973). 129 pp.

Greenway, who now teaches at Westminster Theological Seminary and who has

Annotated Bibliography

been active in overseas missions with the Christian Reformed Church, approaches urban evangelism from "a Calvinist standpoint" (p. ix) and focuses on the role of the church in a changing neighborhood. He advocates a wholistic gospel for the whole person, and gives us some concrete examples of how to combine evangelism and social involvement, especially in chapters IV and V (pp. 65-101).

Haines, J. Harry. *Committed Locally—Living Globally* (Nashville: Abingdon, 1982). 95 pp.

Volume 15 in a seventeen volume series built around the theme "Into Our Third Century," initiated by the General Council on Ministries of the United Methodist Church and prepared for that denomination's bicentennial in 1984. Deals with how United Methodists have responded to the world in evangelism, social concern, and mission. Definitely an "in-house" volume, but honest, open, and hopeful.

Hancock, Robert Lincoln, ed. *The Ministry of Development in Evangelical Perspective* (Pasadena, Calif.: William Carey Library, 1979). 109 pp.

Subtitled, "A Symposium on the Social and Spiritual Mandate." The book is one dozen papers presented to a 1977 symposium, convened by Carl F. H. Henry at Star Ranch in Colorado Springs, Colorado and sponsored by Development Assistance Services, Inc., a subsidiary of World Relief of the National Association of Evangelicals. The papers examine the biblical meaning of sociospiritual development. Reading Carl Henry's closing essay alone would more than justify the book's price.

Harrell, Jr., David Edwin. *Varieties of Southern Evangelicalism* (Macon, Ga.: Mercer University Press, 1981). 114 pp.

Six essays by such men as Martin E. Marty and Samuel S. Hill, Jr., which grew out of the Fourth Annual Hugo Black Symposium held at the University of Alabama in Birmingham in 1979. My pick of the essays is the superb one on Billy Graham by William Martin. Read them all to learn more about one place in the modern world where religion and culture are bonded; and to discern the roots of the new prosperous evangelicalism in the South.

Henry, Carl F. H. *Evangelicals in Search of Identity* (Waco, Tex.: Word Books, Publisher, 1976). 96 pp.

This monograph by evangelicalism's leading theologian originally appeared as ten essays in *Christianity Today*. They are intended by the publisher as a sequel to Henry's 1947 tract, *The Uneasy Conscience of Modern Fundamentalism*. If the 1947 tract was a manifesto of neoevangelicalism and an ardent plea for neoevangelical ethics, then the 1976 tract is an assessment of evangelicals a quarter century afterwards. Henry suggests that in 1976 evangelicals may be farther along the bleak road to becoming "a wilderness cult in a secular society with no more public significance than the ancient Essenes in the Dead Sea caves" (p. 16).

Hessel, Dieter T. *Social Ministry* (Philadelphia: The Westminster Press, 1982). 228 pp.

Evangelism and Social Involvement

A substantive offering on the basic theory and skills for wholistic Christian social ministry, by an informed and experienced executive of the Presbyterian Church U.S.A. Hessel does not take us on another tour of issues. Instead, he makes a careful exploration of a whole strategy of church mission/ministry in response to urgent ethical concerns. Weak on evangelism.

Hinson, E. Glenn. *The Evangelization of the Roman Empire* (Macon, Ga.: Mercer University Press, 1981). 332 pp.

"A study of the contribution which Christianity's major institutional forms (catechumenate and baptism, the Eucharist, disciplinary procedures, scriptures and creeds, and apostolic ministry) made to the winning of the Roman Empire in the first several centuries A.D." (p. 9). Hinson's goal is to depict the role which institutions played in Christianity's evangelistic success. His general conclusion is that early Christianity (up to about 451) achieved its chief goals by means of its total corporate life. He contends "that Christianity spread principally and *normally*, though not exclusively, through the planting of churches" (p. 33). Throws some new light on the historical roots of evangelism and social involvement.

Holmes, Thomas J. and Bryan, Jr., Gainer E. *Ashes for Breakfast* (Valley Forge: The Judson Press, 1969). 127 pp.

A diary of racism in an American church in the deep South—Tattnall Square Baptist Church, Macon, Georgia. Thomas J. Holmes was dismissed by his congregation. A confrontation centered around a young African student who had been converted to Christianity through missionary efforts of churches which now denied him their fellowship. Read it to gain insight into the meaning of prophetic evangelism.

Hudson, Winthrop S. ed. *Walter Rauschenbusch: Selected Writings*, a volume in the series, "Sources of American Spirituality" (New York: Paulist Press, 1984). 252 pp.

Hudson is Professor Emeritus of Church History at Colgate-Rochester Divinity School. He gives us an illuminating introduction to Rauschenbusch. Selections are chosen and edited which show the connection between social justice and Christian piety in the "Father of the Social Gospel." Those interested in the linkages between evangelism and social involvement will find resources here not readily available elsewhere.

Kerans, Partrick. *Sinful Social Structures* (New York: Paulist Press, 1974). 113 pp.

A volume of the Paulist Press series, "Topics in Moral Argument," by a professional theologian and trained economist. Kerans instead of defining sinful social structures describes them, using economic inequality or poverty as exhibit A. His theological reflection has led him to find the mystery of evil as the root of contemporary social problems; but also to the conclusion that Christ's saving grace offers forgiveness for both private and social sin.

Kirk, Andrew. *The Good News of the Kingdom Coming: The Marriage of Evange-*

Annotated Bibliography

lism and Social Responsibility (Downers Grove, Ill.: InterVarsity Press, 1983). 164 pp.

A biblical and kingdom approach in nontechnical language, presenting a challenge to Christians to consider afresh how adequately we are expressing our faith to the real challenges of today. This book will enable us to be more relevant as we look to the third Christian millennium.

Lamb, Matthew L. *Solidarity with Victims: Toward a Theology of Social Transformation* (New York: Crossroad, 1982). 158 pp.

Professor Lamb of Marquette University addresses his theological colleagues and theological communities in this much-documented work. His scholarly volume is "a programmatic study of some of the changes required if we are to do theology in self-critical solidarity with victims" (p. X). The book analyzes some of the methodological tasks which a political theology should undertake if it is to contribute to genuine social transformation.

McNeill, Donald P., Morrison, Douglas A., and Nouwen, Henri J. M. *Compassion: A Reflection on the Christian Life* (Garden City, N. Y.: Doubleday & Co., Inc., 1982). 144 pp.

A book of meditations on suffering with others by three Roman Catholic friends who teach pastoral theology. It is enriched with drawings on compassion done by Joel Filartiga, a medical doctor in Paraguay.

Magnuson, Norris. *Salvation in the Slums: Evangelical Social Work, 1865-1920* (Metuchen, N. J.: The Scarecrow Press, Inc. and The American Theological Library Association, 1977). 299 pp.

A revised doctoral dissertation at the University of Minnesota under Professor Timothy L. Smith. There is a sense in which Magnuson picks up where Smith left off in his *Revivalism and Social Reform*. His story is about the gospel welfare evangelicals, the evangelistic welfare movement, those revivalistic slum workers committed to saving souls; but his thesis is that their extensive welfare activities sprang from their passion for evangelism and personal holiness.

Maney, Thomas. *Basic Communities: A Practical Guide for Renewing Neighborhood Churches* (Minneapolis, Minn.: Winston Press, 1984). 101 pp.

A Roman Catholic priest, who spent twenty-two years as a missionary in Latin America, shares the story of how he and his colleagues have successfully adapted the Latin model and formed 300 basic church communities in middle-class American parishes. Evangelism and social involvement are integrated in this model.

Moberg, David O. *The Great Reversal* (Philadelphia: J. B. Lippincott Co., 1977, rev. ed.). 228 pp.

Subtitled, "Evangelism and Social Concern." Originally published in 1972. The term, "the Great Reversal," comes from Professor Timothy L. Smith, now of Johns Hopkins University. Sociologist Moberg offers a sociohistorical and biblical study primarily for evangelicals, which addresses such questions as: why did

Evangelism and Social Involvement

the evangelical church discontinue its involvement in social concerns? What have been the consequences? Is a commitment to personal evangelism incompatible with an interest in social issues? Chapter 9 describes a wide variety of churches, parachurch groups, and countercultural Christian organizations seeking to reverse the great reversal in their practice of wholistic evangelism and social involvement.

Morris, Leon. *Testaments of Love: A Study of Love in the Bible* (Grand Rapids: William B. Eerdmans Publishing Co., 1981). 298 pp.

A scholarly, up-to-date study on the biblical theme of love. Should be set alongside Nygren's monumental work on *agapē*.

Mouw, Richard J. *Political Evangelism* (Grand Rapids: William B. Eerdmans Publishing Co., 1973). 111 pp.

A Reformed perspective on evangelism in its *political* context. Mouw presents a New Testament case for politically relevant evangelism. He views the church as a "model political community." Firmly grounded in Scripture, this slender volume can especially help conservative evangelical Christians to deal more adequately with such concerns as social justice, racism, and militarism.

Nygren, Anders. *Agape and Eros,* translated by Philip S. Watson (Philadelphia: The Westminster Press, 1953 ed.). 764 pp.

Originally published in three parts between 1932 and 1939, although growing old, still one of the best examples we have of "motif-research." I particularly recommend the reading of this work because of its contrasts between *agape* and *eros* and *nomos,* and because of my treatment of *agapē* in chapter 4.

Oostdyk, Harv. *Step One: The Gospel and the Ghetto* (Basking Ridge, N. J.: SonLife International, Inc., 1983). 342 pp.

An unusual book by a man who loves the poor of our cities. Its poetry, pictures, and practical plans are its strength. The author is a living example of a Christian who bridges the gulf between evangelism and social involvement.

Padilla, C. Rene. *Mission Between the Times* (Grand Rapids: William B. Eerdmans Publishing Co., 1985). 199 pp.

A collection of essays, previously published separately, reflecting the international theological dialogue that has taken place in evangelical circles since the 1974 Lausanne International Congress on World Evangelization; by a Baptist pastor in Buenos Aires, seeking to turn the face of evangelicalism in the direction of a suffering world.

Perkins, John. *Let Justice Roll Down: John Perkins Tells His Own Story* (Ventura, Calif.: Regal Books, 1976). 223 pp.

The inspiring autobiography of the founder of Voice of Calvary Ministries, published in the forty-sixth year of his life. Senator Mark Hatfield called Perkins "nearly a martyr and ... surely a modern saint." This book will help you

Annotated Bibliography

understand why and how Voice of Calvary Ministries puts evangelism and social involvement together.

――――――, ――――――. *A Call to Wholistic Ministry* (St. Louis, Mo.: Open Door Press, 1980). 59 pp.

A booklet spelling out Perkins' vision for wholistic ministry. Contains a succinct biography and history of Perkins and Voice of Calvary Ministries (pp. 5-9). Contends that the gospel is more than proclamation; that it includes human rights also; and that it must be fleshed out by today's church.

――――――, ――――――. *A Quiet Revolution* (Waco, Tex.: Word Books, Publisher, 1976). 226 pp.

Accurately subtitled, "The Christian Response to Human Need . . . a Strategy for Today." Considerable overlapping with the author's *Let Justice Roll Down*. A well-organized, well-written, biblically based, and theologically conservative strategy for Christian community development among poor people—especially blacks in the rural South. Much of the history of Voice of Calvary Ministries up to 1976 will be found here.

――――――, ――――――. *With Justice for All* (Ventura, Calif.: Regal Books, 1982). 211 pp.

Intended as a sequel to the author's *Let Justice Roll Down*. Perkins accurately calls it "a blueprint—a practical strategy by which American evangelicals can do the work of biblical justice in our land." Goes beyond *relief* efforts and concentrates on *development* and *transformation* through the three R's of relocation, reconciliation, and redistribution. There is some repetition of content found in all three of Perkins' earlier books. Perkins is not afraid to take on white evangelicals, the black church, or political liberals. Chapter 11, "The Reconciled Community" (pp. 103-112), is the fullest rationale and vision I have seen for the Voice of Calvary Fellowship church and its relationship to Voice of Calvary Ministries. Chapter 13, "Ten Years Later" (pp. 122-137), brings together all of the ministries of VOC in Mendenhall, Jackson, and New Hebron, Mississippi and takes the reader on a driving (or walking) tour of each as it existed in 1981.

Pinson, Jr., William M. *Applying the Gospel* (Nashville: Broadman Press, 1975). 143 pp.

This is a handbook of suggestions for Christian social action in a local church. It is the most practical aid of its kind that I know. Very well organized and written.

Rauschenbusch, Walter. *Christianity and the Social Crisis* (New York: George H. Doran Co., 1907). 429 pp.

Rauschenbusch saw this book as the payment of a debt he owed to the plain working people of the West Side of New York City where he pastored for eleven years. The kingdom of God theme is dominant. In his mind, "the essential purpose of Christianity was to transform human society into the kingdom of God by regenerating all human relations and reconstituting them in accordance with the will of God" (p. XIII). Readers should put the volume in the context of that time, which Rauschenbusch called "an economic and social revolution." The author used the term "social evangelization" (p. 353) as an answer to the social crisis of his day.

―――――, ―――――. *A Theology for the Social Gospel* (New York: Abingdon Press, 1945). 279 pp.

Rauschenbusch's magnum opus. A restatement of Christian theology in terms of social consciousness by the man whom Reinhold Niebuhr called "the real founder of social Christianity" in America. The book grew out of the Taylor Lectures at Yale School of Religion in 1917; is dedicated to A. H. Strong; and according to the author "is just as orthodox as the Gospel would allow."

Richardson, William J. *Social Action vs. Evangelism: An Essay on the Contemporary Crisis* (South Pasadena, Calif. William Carey Library, 1977). 53 pp.

The booklet argues that evangelism *is* social action, but strangely contends that evangelism does not mean direct involvement in changing social, political, and economic systems.

Samuel, Vinay and Sugden, Chris, eds. *Sharing Jesus in the Two Thirds World* (Grand Rapids: William B. Eerdmans Publishing Co., 1983). 284 pp.

Fourteen papers presented to a conference of evangelical mission theologians from the Two Thirds World in Bangkok, Thailand, March 22-25, 1982. The focus is on Christology, centered around the question: What does it mean to proclaim Jesus Christ in situations of poverty, powerlessness, and oppression?

Scott, Waldron. *Bring Forth Justice* (Grand Rapids: William B. Eerdmans Publishing Co., 1980). 318 pp.

Scott is general secretary of the World Evangelical Fellowship. His book is a substantive, biblically based, theologically conservative treatment of the triangular relationship between mission, disciple making, and social justice. I view its appearance as a sign of hope that evangelicals may be becoming more wholistic in their approach to world evangelization.

Sider, Ronald J., ed. *The Chicago Declaration* (Carol Stream, Ill. Creation House, 1974). 144 pp.

Contains the brief declaration drawn up over the Thanksgiving holiday weekend in 1973; a list of its original signers; the major addresses presented to the Thanksgiving Workshop on Evangelicals and Social Concern gathered in Chicago; and reflections on the document by nine of its original signers. Those making major addresses were William Pannell, Foy Valentine, Paul S. Rees, and John H. Yoder.

―――――, ―――――, ed. *Evangelicals and Development* (Philadelphia: The Westminster Press, 1981). 123 pp.

The papers and findings of a five-day consultation on the theology of development, held in Hoddesdon, England, March 10-14, 1980, sponsored by the Unit on Ethics and Society of the Theological Commission of the World Evangelical

Annotated Bibliography

Fellowship. An evangelical approach toward a theology of social change, and a prelude to what was called WHEATON '83.

Simon, Arthur. *Bread for the World* (Grand Rapids: William B. Eerdmans Publishing Co., 1984 rev. ed.). 219 pp.

A general introduction to world hunger emphasizing the neglected role of public policy; a potpourri of resources for concerned citizens. Originally published in 1975. Offers a workable strategy for individual citizens to alleviate world hunger.

Sine, Tom. *The Church in Response to Human Need* (Monrovia, Calif.: Missions Advanced Research and Communication Center, 1983). 487 pp.

Contains fourteen papers prepared for the conference, I Will Build My Church—WHEATON '83, and particularly for the subconsultation of that meeting on The Church in Response to Human Need. Three of the papers I found weak, one of them both weak and angry. One of them I found wordy and light; but several are excellent, and the others are either very well done or worthy contributions. The book also includes the 1982 Grand Rapids report in its entirety. It puts evangelism and social involvement into a theologically conservative world perspective.

Smith, Glenn C., ed. *Evangelizing Adults* (Wheaton, Ill.: Tyndale House Publishers, Inc., 1985). 409 pp.

Published by Tyndale for the Paulist National Catholic Evangelization Association in Washington, D. C. Written for popular consumption, it is "a presentation of contemporary methods for reaching out to the inactives, the alienated, and the unchurched throughout our nation" (p. 10). Its significance is the wide variety of models and resources which Smith brings together into one volume under the sponsorship of a Roman Catholic evangelistic organization. Those models and resources include local churches and parachurch groups.

Smith, Timothy L. *Revivalism and Social Reform in Mid-Nineteenth-Century America* (New York: Abingdon Press, 1957). 253 pp.

Scholarship of the first rank by a Nazarene scholar who now teaches at Johns Hopkins University. Most of the book comprises The Frank S. and Elizabeth D. Brewer Prize Essay for 1955 by The American Society of Church History. Smith makes a general reevaluation of mid-nineteenth-century Protestantism. The gist of his thesis is that the historical antecedents of the social gospel movement are in the revival measures and perfectionist aspirations which flourished in America between 1840 and 1865—particularly in the cities. "Far, from disdaining earthly affairs, the evangelists played a key role in the widespread attack upon slavery, poverty, and greed," wrote Smith. "They thus helped prepare the way both in theory and in practice for what later became known as the social gospel" (p. 8).

Stott, John. *The Lausanne Covenant: An Exposition and Commentary* (Minneapolis, Minn.: World Wide Publications, 1975). 62 pp.

The Lausanne Covenant was the theological document which came out of the

180
Evangelism and Social Involvement

1974 International Congress on World Evangelization held in Lausanne, Switzerland, under the auspices of the Billy Graham Evangelistic Association. Stott was its primary drafter.

_____, _____. *Christian Mission in the Modern World* (Downers Grove, Ill.: InterVarsity Press, 1975). 128 pp.

An Anglican who has been involved with both ecumenists (World Council) and evangelicals (Lausanne) examines the biblical meaning of mission, evangelism, dialogue, salvation, and conversion. He prioritizes evangelism over everything else (pp. 35-37).

_____, _____. *Involvement: Being a Responsible Christian in a Non-Christian Society* (Old Tappan, N. J.: Fleming H. Revell Co. 1984), 221 pp.

Volume 1 in the Revell Crucial Questions Series. Stott applies the biblical revelation to the pressing issues of the day: the nuclear threat, our human environment, North-South economic inequality, and human rights. The book is his attempt to help evangelicals catch up on their social responsibilities.

Stromberg, Jean, comp. *Mission and Evangelism: An Ecumenical Affirmation* (Geneva: World Council of Churches, 1983). 84 pp.

This is a study guide which includes and is based on the text of the affirmation drawn up by the Commission on World Mission and Evangelism (CWME) of the WCC in July of 1982. Those wanting the uninterrupted text of the document may purchase one from WCC. The document is also printed in the *International Bulletin of Missionary Research*, vol. 7, no. 2, April 1983, pp. 65-71.

Ward, Harry F. *Social Evangelism* (New York: Missionary Education Movement of the United States and Canada, 1915). 145 pp.

An early attempt to interface evangelism and social Christianity. Recognizes the validity and necessity of both individual and social conversion. Makes much of the organic nature of society. Presents some of the most cogent arguments I have read against the idea that you can change the world merely by saving individual souls.

Wilke, Harold H. *Creating the Caring Congregation* (Nashville: Abingdon, 1980). 110 pp.

Guidelines for the congregation wanting to respond to the needs of handicapped persons. Wilke has no hands, but his handicap didn't keep him from writing a very useful book.

The Willowbank Report—Gospel and Culture, Lausanne Occasional Papers No. 2 (Published by the Lausanne Committee for World Evangelization, 1978). 37 pp. paperback.

The official report of a consultation on gospel and culture held at Willowbank, Somerset Bridge, Bermuda, January 6-13, 1978, sponsored by the Lausanne Theology and Education Group of the LCWE.

Annotated Bibliography

Winter, Rebecca J. *The Night Cometh: Two Wealthy Evangelicals Face the Nation* (South Pasadena, Calif.: William Carey Library, 1977). 84 pp.

A documented history of Lewis and Arthur Tappan's involvement in evangelism and social reformation during the nineteenth century. Shows that wealthy, evangelistically minded laymen have not always been lacking in concern for the physical and social needs of the world.

Wirt, Sherwood Eliot. *The Social Conscience of the Evangelical* (New York: Harper & Row, Publishers, 1968). 177 pp.

Wirt was editor of *Decision* magazine when he wrote the book. Carl F. H. Henry called it "A mood-book rather than a text-book." The author uses the needle of love to give us a long overdue evangelical perspective on social responsibility. He illuminates some reasons for evangelical social backwardness and tackles head-on the major issues of the 1960s.

Indexes

Scripture Index

Old Testament

Genesis
  1:1   55
  1:26-27   57
  1:26-31   27
  1:31   55, 153
  3   56-57
  3:9   30
  3:15   30
  3:17-18   58

Exodus
  5:1   30
  19:5-6   147

Numbers
  11:26-30   145
  11:29   147

1 Samuel
  2:1-10   36

Psalms
  8   57
  8:4   57
  8:5-8   57
  19:1-4a 56
  19:4b-6   56
  19:7-11   57
  73:28   55
  136   56
  146:1-10   55

Isaiah
  1:17   110
  9:2   69
  42:8   125
  43:1-13   81
  43:21   147
  44:3   155
  55:11   112
  58:6-9b 135
  61:1-2   31
  61:1-11   13

Jeremiah
  5:7-8   152
  5:11   152
  5:26-28   152-153
  29:7   99

Ezekiel
  18:30   152

Hosea
  1   147
  2   147
  7:8   28

Joel
  2   40
  2:28-29   38

Indexes

Amos
5:24   30, 102

Habakkuk
2:4   31

New Testament

Matthew
5:14-16   69
5:46   65
7:15-23   162
9:35   164
11:2-6   66
12:20   156
16:13-14   145
21:11   145
22:37-40   28, 92
22:38-39   29
22:40   29
23:15   59
25:31-46   16, 34, 35
25:45   35, 64
28   23
28:16-20   27
28:20   29

Mark
1:4   152
1:14-15   152
2:1-12   32
2:27   37
5:1-20   32

Luke
1:46-55   36
3:14   36
4:16-30   13, 31
4:18-19   33, 81
9:49-50   155
10:25-37   16, 64, 135
10:29-37   64, 65
16:19-31   34
24:19   37

John
1:1-3   58
3:16   64

3:18   97
4   116
4:42   147
4:46-54   32
9   32
9:4   165
10:10   108
17:18   145
20:21   81, 92, 145
20:31   33

Acts
1:6-11   81, 90
1:7-8   90
2   40
2:16-21   40
3   42
4:12   125
6   40, 42, 130
6:1-7   146
6:5   146
7   130
8   40, 42, 130
9   41
9:34-35   41-42
9:36   41
10   40
11   40
13:44-52   40
15   40
17:30   152
21:8   42, 130, 146
28:31   40

Romans
1:17   31
8:1   104
8:1-4   102
8:19-22   58
8:21   58

13   39
13:8   92
14:1 to 15:6   156
15:7   156

1 Corinthians
4:20   65
9:22   156
10:23 to 11:1   156
12:3   39
12:14-26   155
13:1-3   66
13:8   64

2 Corinthians
5:6-21   55
5:14   29, 66
5:17   59

Galatians
2:20   112, 121
3:28   41
5:14   92
6:10   64

Ephesians
1:10   59
2:8-9   36
2:10   36
2:14-15   41
2:15   59
4:11   146
4:11-16   145
4:12   86
4:28   36
6:12   61

Philippians
2:11   39

Colossians
1:16   58
1:17   58

2 Timothy
4:5   146

Philemon
4-22   38
16   41

Hebrews
2:3   13
3:1   147

James
1:26-27   36
2:19   161

1 Peter
2:9*b*   147
2:9-10   59, 147
3:15   129

1 John
3:16   63-64
4:2-3   153
4:8   66
4:20-21   92

Revelation
1   55
1:5   147
2   55
5:9-10   59
13   39
21:1   58
21:5   55, 58

Indexes

General Index

Aeneas, 41
agapē, 63-66
Alexander, John F., 148-149
Allen, Horace, 43
Apostles' Creed, 39
Aristides, 125
Augsburger, Myron, 55

Bainton, Roland H., 48
Balint, Ron, 82
Barmen Declaration, 51
Barr, Browne, 20
Barrett, David B., 15
Barth, Karl, 20
Best, Payne, 52
Bethlehem Covenant Church, 84
Birmingham, John D., 125, 126
Blake, William, 66
Boer, Harry R., 59
Boggs, Ray, 87
Bonhoeffer, Dietrich, 51-52, 142
Bronx Baptist Church, Bronx, 81-90
Bronx Shepherds' Restoration Corporation, 87-88

Cabrini-Green Legal Aid Clinic, 99
Cakchiquel, 45
Calley, William Jr., 60, 61
Calvary Bible Church (Burbank, California), 114, 121
Calvin, John, 143
Cambridge, 47
Cannata, Sam and Ginny, 78-79
Cannon, William R., 21
Catholic Worker, 164
Chafin, Kenneth, 162
Chapman, Ian, 98
Chesterton, G. K., 31, 81
Christian Rehabilitation Center (Rebound)
(Charlotte, NC), 102-108, 121-122
Chronister, Keith, 151
Chronos, 137
Church Growth Movement, 44
church planting, 110-111
Clapham Sect, 47-49
Communism, 62
Community Gospel Chapel (Parkchester), 85
community health evangelists, 47
Confessing Church, 51, 52
Continuing Witnessing Training (CWT), 85, 137
Conversion of Structure Approach, 130-132
Cooper, Anthony Ashley, 47
Cornelius, 40
corporate sin, 60-62
Costello, John, 97
Cox, John B., 162
creation, 55-59
cross, 64, 66
cultural mandate, 27-30, 92

Day, Dorothy, 149
decision, 95
denominational heritage, 156-157
development, 18
Dillard, Annie, 139, 140
discipleship, 78
Doddridge, Philip, 48

early church, 38-42
Eisenmann, Tom, 126-127
Emmanuel Gospel (Boston, Mass.), 108-113, 121-122,
  Cooperative Ministires, 108-109
  Pioneer Ministries, 109
Endicott, James, 45, 46

Ephraim, 28
Ethiopian eunuch, 40, 42
Evangelical Council for Financial Accounting, 121
evangelism,
   and ethics, 23, 28
   and intentionality, 15
   and orthodoxy, 161-162
   and structures, 14-15
   and the Holy Spirit, 14-16
   and the kingdom of God, 14
   child, 119
   definition of, 14-16
   demonstration, 86, 88
   issues, 86, 88
   literacy, 162
   of Jesus, 142-143
   open air, 110
   point of need, 135-143
   presence, 97
   prophetic, 145-154
   propositional, 135-138
   renewal, 86
   sweat, 87, 88
evangelism and social responsibility—
their relationship to each other, 20-23
   in the cultural and evangelistic mandates, 27-30
   in the healing ministry of Jesus, 32-33
   in the judgment of the nations scene, 34-35
   in the mission of Jesus, 33
   in the Prophets, 30-31
   in the story of the rich man and Lazarus, 34
Evangelism Explosion (EE), 137
evangelistic mandate, 27-37, 92
Evans, Stanley G., 30

Faith Ministries, 74
Falwell, Jerry, 148
Finney, Charles Grandison, 49, 50, 51

Finneyite Free Churches, 50
First Baptist Church (Brooklyn, New York), 81
First Baptist Church (Kingston, Oklahoma), 150
First Baptist Church (Papillion, Nebraska), 162
Fitzgerald, F. Scott, 155
Ford, Leighton, 20
Four Spiritual Laws, 139
Fowler, Franklin, 44
Fuller, Jim, 75-76
Fundamentalism, morphological, 113

Gary, Raymond, 151
Genovese, Catherine, 158-159
Gentile, 40-41
Gideon New Testament, 74
Glenn, Charlie, 110
Gnostics, 153
God's rainbows, 96-97
Godsey, John, 51
Golden Gate Baptist Theological Seminary, 75
Golden Gate Park, 76
Gordon-Conwell Theological Seminary, 109
gospel tract, 76
Graham, Billy, 63, 102, 146, 147, 148
Graham, Melvin, 102
Graves, Dru, 69-71
group evil, 61

Habakkuk, 31
halfway, house, 74
Hall, Doug and Judy, 113
Hannibal-Lagrange College, 76
Hays, George, 43
Hellenist widows, 42
Hell's Kitchen, 62
Hemingway, Ernest, 60
Hendrix, John, 77-78
Henry, Carl F. H., 21-22
Hernandez, Rudy, 150
Hiebert, Paul, 46

Indexes

Hitler, Adolf, 51-52, 62
Hoehn, Bob, 76-77
Hoge, Dean R., 14
Hogren, Charles, 99
Holocaust, 51
Home Mission Board (of SBC), 84
Hominy Baptist Church, 90-95
Honeywell Avenue Chapel
   (South Bronx), 85

Israel, ancient, 147

James, William, 164
Jesus, 32, 33
Jews, 41
John M. Perkins International
   Study Center, 118
John Paul II, 164
Johnson, Emmett V., 161
Joyce, James, 60

kairos, 137
Kelley, Dean, 14
Kennedy, James, 136
Korea
     Protestant church of, 43
Krass, Alfred, 151

Lane, Henry, 45
Lasalle Street Church
   (Chicago, Illinois), 99
Lausanne Committee, 13, 19
Lawrence, D. H., 60
Lax, W. H., 163
Lazarus, 34
Leitch, Wayne, 119
Leslie, William, 99
Lewis, Chuck, 128
Line, Hubert, 71-72
Lowell, James Russell, 41
love, 56
Lumpkin, Ronald and Charlotte, 110
Luther, Martin, 157
Lynn, Torie, 65

MacArthur, Jack, 121
Magnificat, 36
Manley, Basil, Jr., 78
Marney, Carlyle, 157
Marcion, 153
Maryknoll Order, 130-131
Masefield, John, 29
mass evangelism, 13
Maston, T. B., 17
McBride, John, 131
McGavran, Donald, 13, 15, 44
medical missions, 78
Medieval Christendom, 40
Methodists, 47
migrants, 70
Milner, Isaac, 48
Moberg, David O., 14
modern missions, 42-47
Mollenkott, Virginia Ramey, 135
Moody Bible Institute, 112
Moseley, Winston, 159
Moses, 30
Mt. Washington Baptist Church, 77-78
Mulberry Baptist Church
   (Charlotte, NC), 99-100
Murle, 78-79

neognosticism, 153
Never-On-Rainy-Friday-the-
   Thirteenth Approach, 127-128
New Hartford Baptist Church, 76
Newton, John, 105
Niebuhr, Richard, 151
Niemoeller, Martin, 52, 62
Night Ministry
   (San Francisco, California), 128
Nightingale, Florence, 69
Nixon, Richard, 145

Onesimus, 41
orthopraxy, 162

Palau, Luis, 145
Paraquay
     first Baptist hospital in, 44

Paul, 30, 39-40
Peck, M. Scott, 61
People's Development, Inc. (PDI), 117
Perkins, John, 29, 60, 114-121
Peter, 41
Philemon, 41
Philip, 42
Pine Grove Baptist (Rockingham, NC), 96
Pitt, William, 48
polarization, 130
poverty, 60, 131
protracted meetings, 49

Raeford, Angela "Cookie," 65
Ranscheart, B. J., 85
Rastafarians, 85
Rauschenbusch, Walter, 33, 55, 60, 62
reconciliation, 115
redemption, 57
redistribution, 116
Reed, Phillip K., 120
Reese, Pee Wee, 158
Reformed Bible College (Grand Rapids, Michigan), 19
rehabilitation, 18
relief, 18
relocation, 115
revivalism, 49
Rice, Bobby, 151
Richardson, Bobby, 73
Risky-Deed-and-Word Approach, 126-127
Roberts, Oral, 148
Robinson, Cecilia, 83
Robinson, Jackie, 158
Roman citizens, 39
Rowland, Stanley, 46
Royal Ambassadors, 72

Saint John Lutheran Church, 86
Saint Theresa of Avila, 59, 64
Salvation Center, 74
Samaritans, 40

San Quentin, 75-76
sanctification, 13
Sands, George M., 82
Second Great Awakening, 49-51
Shaftesbury, Lord, 47, 49
Shepherds' Restoration Corporation (South Bronx), 87-88
Shriver, Donald W., 39, 41
Simpson, Samuel G., 81-90
sin, 59-63
slavery, 41, 48
Smith, Timothy, 13, 51
social gospel, 62-63
social ministry and social action
 and the church, 17-18
 definition of, 16
 relationship to fundamentalism, 17
 terminology, 18-19
Sogaard, Viggo, 128
Sojourners, 150
South Carolina University, 72
Southern Baptist Convention
 Brotherhood Commission, 44
 Foreign Mission Board, 44
 Home Mission Board, 44
Southern Baptist Theological Seminary, The, 78
Southern Baptists, 44
Specialization Approach, 129-130
Stalin, 62
Stanley, Don, 72-75
Stevenson, Jim, 151
Stott, John R. W., 29, 129-130
Stroud, Linwood, 106
Sweazey, George, 81

Tabitha, 41
Third Baptist Church (St. Louis, Missouri), 97-99
Thompson, Vincent, 83
Thriftco, 117-118
Townsend, Cameron, 45
Traditional Rescue Mission Approach, 125-126

Indexes

Truth, Sojourner, 157
Tucker, Lemuel S., 114, 120
Tuttle, Wayne, 96

U.C.-J.C. Approach, 128-129
United States Army, 75
Upper Room Jesus Compassionate Ministry (Kansas City, Missouri), 125

Vacation Bible School, 75
Vatican II, 131
VOC Family Health Center, 117
Voice of Calvary Fellowship Church, 120
Voice of Calvary Ministries (Jackson, Mississippi), 114-121
volunteer labor, 71

Wade-Eden Chapel (Northeast Bronx), 85

Walker, Alan, 161
Wallis, Jim, 149
Walton, Dave, 74
Ward, Harry F., 50
Weekley, Gordon, 103-108
Werham, Dr. C. Fred, 92-95
Wesley, John, 47
West, Rebecca, 60
Whitefield, George, 47
Wilberforce, William, 47, 48
Wilson, Grady, 102
Wirt, Sherwood Eliot, 13, 36, 42, 143
witchcraft, 45
Women's Missionary Union, 44
World Council of Churches, 13
World Evangelical Fellowship, 19
Wycliffe Bible Translators, 45, 79

Yew, Lee Kuan, 158
Youngren, J. Alan, 18